THE STRATEGIC ACCOUNTANT

Why Accountants Should Learn to Juggle

JOHN HALE

www.halecg.com

Copyright © 2024 by John Hale. All rights reserved.

Published by Hale Consulting Group
15 Manning Street
South Brisbane 4101 Australia
www.halecg.com

This book or any portion thereof may not be reproduced or used in any manner whatsoever without the express written permission of the author.

Limit of Liability/Disclaimer of Warranty: While the publisher and author have used their best efforts in preparing this book, they make no representations or warranties regarding the accuracy or completeness of the contents of this book and expressly disclaim any implied warranties of merchantability or fitness for a particular purpose. No warranty may be created or extended by sales representatives or written sales materials. The publisher and author are not acting as advisors in this book.

This book and the content provided herein are simply for educational purposes and do not in any way take the place of business advice from a professional advisor, be that strategic, financial, legal or otherwise. The information and strategies contained herein may not be suitable for your situation. This book includes non-factual models and metaphors from the author's life and narratives and ideas adapted from many sources. All effort has been made to ensure that the content provided in this book is inspiring and helpful for readers. However, this book is not an exhaustive treatment of the subjects contained within it. The author assumes no liability for losses or damages due to the information provided. You are responsible for your own choices, actions, and results.

Illustrations: John Hale
Book Design: Jana Rade

SECOND EDITION
Paperback: ISBN 978-0-6486590-4-4
E-Book: ISBN 978-0-6486590-5-1

 A catalogue record for this book is available from the National Library of Australia

Over the years, my children have reminded me that we all enjoy the moments that accompany a bedtime story. Before we slumber, enlightening tales free our thoughts and offer strategies for a brighter tomorrow.

This book is dedicated to Rebecca, Claire, Lauren and Lachlan

CONTENTS

INTRODUCTION

The Strategy Guy	3
The King and the Seeds	5
Brief History of Accounting	6
The Strategic Accountant	9
Don't Wobble	11

CHAPTER ONE - ACCOUNTANTS SHOULD LEARN TO JUGGLE

The Imitation Game	16
The Art of Juggling	19
10,000 Hours	21
Juggling Numbers	22
Juggling Rewards	24

CHAPTER TWO - ANALYSING THE PAST

Deloitte	38
EY	41
KPMG	43
PwC	46
Sarbanes-Oxley	48

CHAPTER THREE - MANAGING THE PRESENT

Management Accounting	59
Quality Management	62
Five Whys	64
Fixed Costs Aren't	65
Activity Based Costing	67

CHAPTER FOUR - CREATING THE FUTURE

Keeping Score	80
Secrets to Growth	82
Pareto Effects	85
Scale	87
Post-Strategy Audits	91

CHAPTER FIVE - CULTIVATING A STRATEGIC MINDSET

Industry Analysis	103
Cost Leadership	106
Differentiation	108
Focus	110
Right-Sizing	113

CHAPTER SIX - LEADING STRATEGY

Leading the City	125
Culture Eats Strategy	127
Five Dysfunctions	129
Leading Strategy	132
Writing a Strategy Note	136

CONTENTS

FUTURE PROOF YOUR FIRM

Capability Quiz	150
Capability Score	152

CONCLUSION

Off with the Fairies	156
Speaking Freely	159
The Return of the King	161
Bridging Failure	163
The Edge of Tomorrow	164

APPENDICIES   167

ENDNOTES   185

ACKNOWLEDGEMENTS   193

ABOUT THE AUTHOR   195

INTRODUCTION

The conference session was nearly over.

I raised my hand to request the microphone.

I wanted to ask Michael Porter, the father of modern strategy, a question about shared value and the importance of the natural environment.

A baseball-capped mic runner headed towards my seat in the auditorium to allow me to ask my question.

That was fifteen years ago. Porter had shared the stage with revolutionary thinker Malcolm Gladwell and jovial storyteller Apple co-founder Steve Wozniak.[1]

Today, I speak from the stage and write books on strategy. I wrote this book, The Strategic Accountant, for accountants.

Why accountants, you might ask?

Because in this era of aging populations, global warming, economic upheaval, advancing automation, artificial intelligence (AI) and artificial general intelligence (AGI), accountants need strategy skills to navigate their digital future and decide on the best mix of services.

On the whole, accountants tend to be conservative and take very few risks. They are more likely to speculate about life than have 'skin in the game'. The accounting conferences I speak at are often virtual or are held at seaside resorts, peppered with tennis courts and nearby parasailing activities. Delegates rarely leave the safe confines of the auditorium, their room or the pool deck. Lawyers appear to take more risks. Lawyers conference at wineries and venture out for wobbly rounds of golf.

By contrast, medical conferences held in Italian ski resorts can be downright dangerous. After-lunch, half-inebriated surgeons traverse freshly carved moguls with chianti topped bellies and usually finish their week with injuries to their hands, knees, heads and sometimes all three! The subject of strategy is lost on doctors, but not lawyers. The lawyers sit to one side, cheering-on the hapless accountants, with at times unethical and morally questionable advice.

Some doctors, lawyers and business-people have been prepared to seek out less ethical accountants to divert income and avoid tax. Because of this, I felt it time to offer accountants some ways to become more strategic and ethical. I would like to add that I know many accountants who are highly ethical as well as being excellent skiers. As far as being an accountant is concerned, they are perfect as they are.

However, like all people, who are already perfect, accountants could always do with a little improvement.

INTRODUCTION

THE STRATEGY GUY

At conferences, I motivate accountants and leaders to stop being spectators and create their best future. In my work as a strategic advisor, I help firms juggle three different time frames.

The Past.
The Present.
The Future.

Sometimes, when asked what their father does, my children say, "My Dad is the Strategy Guy."

As the Strategy Guy, my purpose is to be one of the wisest people in the room. Indeed, facilitating a strategy session with a knowledgeable executive group and three years of financials often requires me to ask three questions.

What is going on here?
What are your options?
What will you do?

I nearly became a strategy guy twenty-five years ago when Boston Consulting Group (BCG) invited me to travel the world with them. But there was a catch. This option meant I would only see my children two weeks per year. I dreamt of being a good father and a strategy guy. I chose to reject one role and focus on the other.

THE STRATEGIC ACCOUNTANT

I chose well.

Today my four beautiful, intelligent and ethically astute children are launched. Now, at last, I am The Strategy Guy. "Never give up on your dreams. Whatever you can do or dream you can, begin it. Boldness has genius, power, and magic in it."[2]

When each of my children reached the magical age of three, they began forming causal links between the past, present and future. At that time, I asked them the same three questions.

What is going on here?
What are your options?
What will you do?

I enjoyed supporting their autonomy, curiosity and ethical behaviour. This worked until they were enrolled in the education system.

Once at school, my children changed. Institutional conformity stifled their precious uniqueness and ability to imagine. At the time, J.K Rowling was a great help. Before school, we'd re-enact Order of the Phoenix scenes between Hagrid and Harry.[3]

"You are a wizard, Harry!"
"It's changing out there. Just like last time."
"There's a storm coming, Harry. And we all best be ready."

Evenings gave us time for the magic of Harry Potter, cuddles, backrubs, songs and spiritual bedtime tales. My daughter Claire fondly named

INTRODUCTION

these tales *sushi stories*, as some came from the mystical Islamic Sufi tradition. Each colourful account contained a moral and helped the children sleep peacefully. We each had our favourite *sushi stories*. Sometimes the children asked me to retell The King and the Seeds.[4]

THE KING AND THE SEEDS

Once there was a widower King with three children.

The eldest, Boris, was a fearful outspoken chap. The second eldest, Donald, was a loud, angry brat. The youngest, Jacinda, was a thoughtful girl.

One day, the King summoned his children and said, "I am going on a journey. When I return, I will name one of you to be my successor."

He continued, "I will give each of you a bag of seeds to care for in my absence."

The next day the King handed each child a bag of seeds and departed.

Boris took his seeds to the Palace Treasury and locked them away in an iron vault for safekeeping. Like a responsible auditor, Boris wanted to account for every last seed.

Donald decided to trade his seeds at the local marketplace for gold coins. Like an optimistic trader, Donald wanted to take his chances with time.

Jacinda planted her seeds in the surrounding countryside. Like a long-term investor, Jacinda appreciated the strategic role seeds played in building a bridge to the future.

The future always beckons. Nobody is powerful enough to slow or stop the march of time.

If we are like Jacinda, we may realise that time can be a powerful ally.
If we are like Donald, we may try to bargain with time.
If we are like Boris, we may attempt to turn back time.

The future always beckons. Time and technology keep advancing. Nobody is powerful enough to stop the sands of time.

Accountants and leaders that stick their heads in the sand will be left behind.

BRIEF HISTORY OF ACCOUNTING

Seed-planting farmers first introduced bean-counting near the sandy deserts of ancient Babylon to *audit* harvests.[5] Farmers analysed activities to capture *operational efficiencies*. At the same time, traders

INTRODUCTION

used notes of exchange and numbering systems for *taxation* purposes in the temple economies of Mesopotamia.

Two thousand years ago, at the time of Roman Emperor Augustus, the degree of accounting information at the Emperor's disposal could account for the spoils of war. Generals made *return on investment* calculations to decide which invasions to fund.[6]

In eighth-century Persia, the Quran required that Muslims calculate their indebtedness to God.[7] Executors utilised *double-entry accounting* for the thorny problems of wealth accounting and inheritance. By the tenth century, these bookkeeping systems found their way into Europe's wealthy banks.

By the fourteenth century, Italy's banking centres had amassed great fortunes, thanks to wealth accounting methods. Merchants who did not maintain accurate records of inventories and neglected to audit their books were at *risk of theft* by employees and suppliers.

During the fifteenth century, the Church deployed accounting methods to facilitate what many now recognise as *theft on a large scale*. The Vatican secured German printing technology to issue countless invoices to believers to collect indulgences and tributes.[8]

By the sixteen-hundreds and seventeen-hundreds, bookkeepers printed financial records that were split into *management accounting* statements for internal decision-making and *financial accounting* statements to disclose activities to investors.

By the eighteen-hundreds, regulations for businesses created a growing need for auditors to verify financial statements *independently*. This growing need for auditing gave birth to *chartered accounting* in Scotland, 'the land of the brave' and 'the fair folk'.

In Scotland, chartered accountants belonged to the same associations as solicitors, and both professions regularly *referred* and shared clients. Soon after, the worldwide proliferation of limited liability companies highlighted the issues of inventory valuations, business valuations and asset depreciations. Accountants rapidly became an integral part of banking, finance and commerce.

By the late 1800s, Queen Victoria granted royal charters to the Glasgow Institute of Accountants and Actuaries, the Edinburgh Society of Accountants and the Institute of Chartered Accountants.[9] As membership grew, institutes created *examinations* for admission to raise accountancy's status and exclusivity. Soon after, the American Institute of Certified Public Accountants was established to set similar ethical and auditing *standards*.

The twentieth century saw the meteoric rise of Arthur Anderson, KPMG, EY, PwC and Deloitte, which were *consolidations* of two dozen original accounting firms from the UK, America, Holland, Germany, Canada and Japan.[10]

The twenty-first century has delivered the *autonomous accountant* – a secure, reliable, analytical, networked, insightful, overseeing and transparently auditable AI system.[11] Autonomous accountants will usurp traditional accountants, unless accountants have a strategy for

INTRODUCTION

their future. Another recent entrant is the *carbon accountant*, a strategic mix of human and artificial intelligence that tracks individual company progress toward net zero carbon emissions.

THE STRATEGIC ACCOUNTANT

Today KPMG, EY, PwC and Deloitte are thought-leading consulting firms with sideline accounting practices at arms-reach. Each eclipses the combined earnings of strategy firms Bain & Co, BCG and McKinsey & Co.

The top four have operated as Strategic Accountants for some time. But here's the rub. Just because a firm can do something, that does not make it right. The strategist's objective is to help their client maximise value. The accountant's role is to present a set of accounts that reflect the true state of the business.

As a strategist, I find having an accurate set of accounts for a client's most recent three years extremely valuable. With the figures on hand, this helps me with strategy work for boards and CEOs. Some CEOs aim to pay investors regular dividends and re-invest profits. Other CEOs have a healthy appetite for sky-rocketing stock valuations.

Because double-entry accounting can classify assets, liabilities and cash flows in various ways, accountants can often find themselves supporting a less than ethical CEO's reporting and tax avoidance preferences.

By contrast, the decision to become a Strategic Accountant should be an ethical one. The belief that one can faithfully serve more than one master is often flawed. Conflicts-of-interest are an everyday occurrence where accounting firms help set up tax avoiding offshore companies for clients whilst advising governments on raising tax revenue. Such conflicts should raise the hairs on the back of anyone's neck. One day, such unethical juggling of tasks by accountants will come to an end.

The decision to become a Strategic Accountant requires patience. Recently, partners in one of the top four accounting firms engaged a colleague, Robert, to teach them about strategy. Robert had them work on a business case which involved taking a popular Australian clothing and lifestyle brand to the United States. As the apparel market is huge in the US, these partners believed entering the US market was a great strategic move.

Once my colleague explained why the move would fail, they realised they had very little understanding of American apparel customers and the market's dynamics.

These partners ignored vital facts in the business case. Facts that illustrated why ventures by other Australian labels bombed in the States. Upon realising their inexperience, the partners declared that they were not very good at strategy. One partner wryly shared they felt comforted by the thought that even if the venture bombed, their firm had a good chance of winning the resultant insolvency and administration work.

INTRODUCTION

I believe this ingrained self-serving conflict of interest is the 'elephant in the room'. The key learning here is that failing at anything the first few times, is not a reason to give up. Had my children taken this approach, they would never have learned to roller-skate, surf or ride a bike.

DON'T WOBBLE

As my children grew up, they would feel conflicted between life's choices. Wanting to be with friends, cleaning their room or completing a science project all beckoned. Sometimes they tried to juggle having a friend over to 'help' with the science project or 'keep them company' while they cleaned. I would say, "Sitting sit. Standing stand. Don't wobble."

I encouraged them to be loyal to one choice. A good strategy is similar. The right things get done in a timely fashion once other distractions and roles fall away.

Becoming a Strategic Accountant will mean becoming proficient at strategy whilst moving away from traditional accounting and audit roles, now being automated. Audit and accounting roles concern themselves with the task of analysing the past and presenting a clear financial picture. Today, automation and AI do this for us. The best accountants keep evolving to remain relevant and create added value.

With automation and AI taking over audit, compliance and tax accounting roles in society, we will see more and more dashboard apps providing businesses with actionable efficiency measures and real-time updates.

As more accountants help their clients manage the present and create the future, they will learn to do a three-way juggle. A Strategic Accountant is an accountant that has learnt to juggle three distinct time frames. Strategic Accountants are able to have value-driven conversations within their own firms and with their clients to help them learn from the past, manage the present and create the future.

Some accountants may find this book challenging. Like a court jester, I will expose the powerful players who would rather secure the lion's share of the gold, than share it. I will juggle vital issues like ethics, automation, AI, gender discrimination, cost accounting, quality management, competition, leadership, culture and of course, strategy.

The Strategic Accountant aligns with six capabilities in the Chartered Accountants Australia and New Zealand (CAANZ) Capabilities for Accounting – A model for the future.[12] This book may be of assistance to accountants in the professional development areas of technology fluency; ethics and integrity; critical thinking and judgement; adaptive mindset; future focus and leading others.

If you are a leader or a parent, you are already on track to becoming an accomplished juggler. Family is not an important thing. It is everything. At one stage in my life, I was broke. It was then, I learned that a truly rich man is one whose children run into his arms, even when his hands are empty.

INTRODUCTION

Half the pages in this book are empty. That is because I am inviting you to write in this book. I want you to capture your ideas and the strategies that excite and interest you. Most books are one-way monologues. I have designed this book to be a two-way dialogue - so you can be engaged and interact with the material.

One-half of this book contains a collection of frameworks, ideas, processes, stories and suggested activities. The other half of the book is designed to capture and juggle your diagnosis, diagrams, deliberations, discoveries and doodles.

Right now, you may be deliberating on the future role of an accountant and what capabilities they will require? To help answer this question, you can also use this book as a reflective journal.

This book will show you how to become a Strategic Accountant and why accountants should learn to juggle.

CHAPTER ONE

ACCOUNTANTS SHOULD LEARN TO JUGGLE

ACCOUNTANTS SHOULD LEARN TO JUGGLE

Would you rather live in the past or the future?

Your answer may help with your decision to become a Strategic Accountant. It's also a trick question. We always live in the present.

We recall the past, but we can create the future.

Today, businesses and accountants are building more and more bridges to the future with Artificial Intelligence (AI). Activities that are repetitive and predictable, like traditional accounting, keep being subsumed by increasingly smarter, faster and cheaper forms of AI.

In 1950, Alan Turing, a young British polymath, created the future of AI.[13] Turing's humble life is the subject of a brilliant movie titled *The Imitation Game*, starring Benedict Cumberbatch and Keira Knightley.

THE IMITATION GAME

From humble beginnings, AI has become a megatrend. I use the term megatrend to refer to significant patterns that will not be changing anytime soon. When strategy aligns with things that are not

CHAPTER ONE: ACCOUNTANTS SHOULD LEARN TO JUGGLE

changing, it succeeds. When we bet on less certain things, success can ellude us.

Success comes from betting on megatrends, such as ageing populations, surging urbanisation, the rising middle class, global warming, water scarcity, AI.

GPT's evolution as a 'bot' is a good example of a megatrend.

Me: Morning GPT

GPT: Good morning! How can I assist you today?

Me: Please review Apple's 2023 financial reports and calculate their quick ratio, ROA and debt ratio

GPT: Quick Ratio: 1.02 - This suggests that for every dollar of current liabilities, Apple has $1.02 in easily liquidated assets, indicating good short-term financial health.

Return on Assets (ROA); 9.59% - This means that Apple generates a return of 9.59 cents for every dollar of assets it owns, showcasing efficient use of its assets to generate profits.

Debt to Equity Ratio: 3.77 - This ratio indicates that Apple has $3.77 in liabilities for every dollar of shareholders' equity, reflecting the company's financial leverage and reliance on debt financing relative to its equity.

When Apple's Steve Wozniak had his turn at the conference, he explained that within a few decades, as devices take care of more and more things, AI would outpace human intelligence. Wozniak explained that in time software would think faster than people, and eventually, smart technology would get rid of 'slow humans' to help companies run more efficiently.

He was right. The role of technology in finance, reporting, compliance and management accounting keeps evolving. In the last thirty years, when governments introduced taxes for capital gains, goods and services and fringe benefits, many accountants were lured away from traditional advisory work.

Soon, governments will take this massive tax compliance work away from accountants. Bookkeeping and traditional accounting functions, including tax reporting, are being swallowed up by advances in automation and AI. To survive and evolve, accountants must rekindle their advisory flame.

In recent years, with evolving ethics and better regulation in the tech space, Wozniak is less afraid. He now believes that human 'intuition' will provide the safety net needed to prevent computers from taking over. More positively, he now shares that AI systems will need to juggle, "They're going to be smarter than us, and if they're smarter than us, they'll realise they need us."[14]

CHAPTER ONE: ACCOUNTANTS SHOULD LEARN TO JUGGLE

THE ART OF JUGGLING

When someone first learns to juggle, there is no recognisable pattern.

Tossed balls spend less time being caught and more time on the ground.

Strategic Accountants are accomplished jugglers. They ensure their firm and their clients' businesses keep three balls in the air. They have a 'virtuous pattern' of understanding the past, managing the present and creating the future.

Understanding which customer patterns are predictable makes the task of strategy straightforward. Successful firms know the answer to the question, "What out there is not changing?" This is at the heart of Amazon's virtuous approach to strategy.

Once Amazon identifies a virtuous consumer pattern, they keep scaling-up their capability and capacity in that space until they dominate it. For example, Amazon realised on-line shopping, books, free-shipping, subscriptions, streamed movies, global logistics and cloud storage are all here to stay. Amazon juggles the past, present and future by deploying AI within its operations, products and services.

The physical act of juggling increases our intelligence. Juggling connects less-connected areas of the brain. Juggling a three-ball cascade is a rewarding pursuit and offers a cascade of benefits. If you don't have access to juggling balls, you can learn to juggle by finding three tennis balls and following these three steps.

Step 1. Throw and catch one ball from one hand to the other.

> Toss a ball from your waist level to a point 30 cm over your head and in-line with your opposite shoulder. Reverse direction and repeat. Left to right, right to left. Repeat until confident.

Step 2. Now start with a ball in each hand.

> Toss one ball from your waist level to a point 30 cm over your head and in-line with your opposite shoulder. The moment the first ball reaches its highest point, toss the second ball in your opposite hand from your waist to a point 30 cm over your head and in-line with your original shoulder. Just after the second ball is thrown from your hand, that same hand catches the first ball. Soon after that, the second ball is caught by the original throwing hand. Repeat until confident.

Step 3. Now place two balls in one hand and one in the other.

> Repeat the process from Step 2, making sure the initial ball tossed always comes from the hand with two balls. With a three-way toss, aim for three tosses (right, left, right) and catches in a row. Then four. Then Five. Then Six. etc.

World-famous juggler Enrico Rastelli, was born into a circus family. Despite being highly proficient at acrobatics, at thirteen, Enrico saw his future in juggling.[15] He practised juggling tirelessly for six years. Practising a new business or life skill over and over for years can dramatically increase our chances of success.

CHAPTER ONE: ACCOUNTANTS SHOULD LEARN TO JUGGLE

Within a few short years, like Enrico, perhaps millions of accountants, once highly proficient at the acrobatics of accounting, could be in search of a new act. Making the shift from trusted accountant to a trusted strategic advisor might feel daunting at first. However, with practise, most people can master just about anything.

Once Enrico had mastered juggling, he kept on learning. Enrico could juggle multiple objects while balancing objects on his head. His world record numbers for juggling remained unbeaten until recently. His hours of practice made Enrico a master of combination tasks, being able to juggle six plates while spinning a hoop around one foot and skipping a rope that was spun by an assistant.

10,000 HOURS

Back at the conference, I skipped the lunch queues to listen to Malcolm Gladwell share the 10,000-hour rule from his book, *Outliers*.[16] Gladwell claimed it took 10,000 hours of practice to achieve mastery of a complex skill. This was the reason why Bill Gates became so good at computer programming and why the Beatles performed so sweetly.

However, 10,000 hours of practice can be bittersweet if the wrong skill sequence is being mastered. Having a good teacher can be just as important as practice. As a former regional basketball champion, I taught my son Lachlan the most important skills of the game. This included spatial awareness, 'killer' handles, shooting step-back threes, free-throws and relentless boxing out in defence. As my son's practice time approaches 10,000 hours, he is on-track to play national league.

Enrico Rastelli's father, who was an accomplished juggler himself, taught Enrico juggling and helped cultivate his son's career. In China, juggling was an art performed by masterful warriors. One warrior, Xiong Yiliao, once juggled nine balls in front of his troops on a battlefield.[17] His display of skill was conferred upon his entire army, and the opposing army fled.

Succeeding with software, music, sport, armed combat, juggling, and strategy is not straight forward. Bill, John, Paul, George, Ringo, Lachlan, Yiliao, Enrico, and I have all discovered it takes a lot of practice.

Records show that Enrico Rastelli had the best juggling numbers. Accountants are also proficient at juggling numbers.

JUGGLING NUMBERS

When it comes to analysing the past for reporting and compliance purposes, many accountants already juggle numbers quite well. The interpretation and application of Generally Accepted Accounting Principles (GAAP) and evolving taxation provisions often vary depending on the client's circumstances. This interpretive aspect usually earns the accountants the 'creative' label.

CHAPTER ONE: ACCOUNTANTS SHOULD LEARN TO JUGGLE

As most clients do not understand GAAP or taxation law, their accountant's otherworldly work seems to border at times on the magical. Whenever the available numbers don't add up the way we'd like, accounting wizards are needed.

As an undergraduate 'computer wizard' in the early eighties, I completed summer contracts in the accounts departments of the local fishing cooperative and a multinational petroleum corporation. I used VisiCalc and Lotus 123 spreadsheets to help the fish co-op record weights of crates and track down worker theft.

As a COBOL and SQL programmer, I converted the petroleum corporation's refinery financial records to enable a transfer from one computer system to a new one. I generated a backup ledger and set of accounts before the conversion, and the refinery operated their accounts payable on a manual system during the conversion period.

Once I had transferred the records over to the new system, I generated a new ledger and set of accounts to check my work. As there were accounting errors in the old system, these were replicated in the new system after my data conversion exercise. However, the new computer mysteriously changed some historical amounts in the conversion process due to new automated statement features.

The before and after statements were encouraging but not a perfect match. I then combed back through files of completed paper invoices and remittance notes to track some incorrect payments. As some invoices had been lost or damaged, I contacted the contracting firms for the correct figures. For those contractors that no-longer existed,

I made reasonable estimates about the historical amounts paid to contractors based on the hours worked and the services provided.

I reported all estimated amounts to my supervisor and the external auditors from an accounting firm whose name was not the same as the auditor on the corporation's annual report. These auditors kept irregular hours, did very little work, and filed a faultless compliance report on the new system after two weeks. Their report was not accurate. In my mind, these auditors should have disclosed the accounting irregularities and my estimates to the petroleum company's refinery management.

JUGGLING REWARDS

The fish co-op manager was so happy with the spreadsheets, he paid me double on the spot. By comparison, my hourly rate for Friday nights and weekends as a restaurant waiter and bartender began looking a little fishy. Like accounting partners, I learned the more money I could make or save a client, the higher the rewards.

My refinery supervisor congratulated me and rewarded me for an excellent job. My reward was to be transferred to a plush new location in the refinery. I spent the remaining two weeks of my contract upstairs on the executive floor, learning how to drive the corporation's under-utilised ten-million-dollar computer-aided design system. To my delight, that

CHAPTER ONE: ACCOUNTANTS SHOULD LEARN TO JUGGLE

system had a flight simulator program as part of the operating system. Once I had reported the accounting problems, just like the auditors, I was paid to look elsewhere. In time, I learnt that all auditors are paid to look, and many are paid to look away.

If you are too young to remember Enron, it is a "getting paid to look away" story worth reading.[18] Alas, since the heady days of Enron and their accounting firm Arthur Anderson, the practice of being paid to look the other way has continued in the accounting profession. Today, however, with the increasing digitisation of global financial transactions and financial regulation, outside parties can audit payments predictably in real-time for reporting and compliance purposes.

Auditing will always have a role to play, even in Rome. Former Vatican treasurer George Pell said upon commencing his role that unless the world's smallest state tamed its ballooning debts, it would eventually "go broke". Pell's reformation of Rome's financial affairs encountered resistance from corrupt Vatican officials, led by Cardinal Giovanni Becciu.

Beccui forced out the external auditors brought in by Pell and the Vatican's first Auditor General. Eventually, Pope Francis fired Becciu, accusing him of nepotism and embezzlement. Becclu was caught using Vatican money to purchase a luxury property in London. Soon after that, Pell said, "I think we are in a much, much better place than we were", when commenting on the reform of Vatican finances, including new computer-based accounting and audit controls.[19]

The fiscal strength of the Vatican may still be uncertain. But death and taxes are certain!

Unless you have a savvy accountant.

Accountants, often egged on by lawyers, wield an exotic array of tools like accruals, amortisations, advances, book values, asset sale and leasebacks, capital losses, depreciation, donations, endowments, exemptions, golden parachutes, offshore wire accounts, black budgets, tax shelters, tax shifts, umbrella companies, vesting and write-offs. Indeed, accountants can achieve tax minimisation, but not everlasting life.

As the biggest accounting firms become more affluent from perfecting tax minimisation for their clients, it seems governments are building less than perfect software programs to help detect tax evasion. In late 2020, a software program failed within an Australian government financial intelligence agency responsible for identifying money laundering, organised crime and tax evasion. A coding error in the agency's computer reported the Vatican had wired more than 40,000 transfers worth AU$2.3 billion from Rome to Australia.

The Vatican auditors claimed the amount was only AU$9.5 million. By 2021, the agency uncovered the system error, which cast into doubt their previous institutional money laundering finding against Australian bank, Westpac. Westpac paid the most significant fine in Australian corporate history. Westpac paid AU$1.3 billion to settle the case brought by the agency.[20] It seems that Westpac may have unfairly lost its Chairman, CEO, market leadership position, commercial reputation and billions in future earnings due to glitches in computer code.

Like Australia and the UK, governments worldwide are paying billions to the world's top four accounting firms to advise on policy relating to raising tax revenue. Indeed, with a portfolio of services, like audit, tax, consulting and now legal, each of the top four is proof that accountants can learn to juggle. In recent years, the top four accounting firms have advised the tax office whilst helping corporate CEOs to circumvent tax regulations.[21]

Such greedy and unethical dilemmas create a fine line, over which most accountants typically don't go. Nevertheless, accountants do fuel the widening gap between the tax-minimised and profit-maximised corporations and the real wages of everyday employees.

This creates a future with a more significant tax burden on the average employee and governments. Meanwhile, global debt continues to rise. And as we will soon see, the Two-Hundred-Billion-Pound-Gorilla in the Room keeps growing.

CAPABILTY ONE

TECHNOLOGY FLUENCY

How intelligent is your firm?

Strategic Accountants realise that postponing their digital transformation puts them at further risk of obsolescence.

On the blank pages opposite, make a list of all the automated systems and artificial intelligence your firm uses.

Examples include adding machines, calculators, spreadsheets, optical character recognition, voice recognition, handwriting to text, MYOB, Xero, Microsoft 365, SAP, ERP systems, HubSpot, OpenAI Apps, government connect', 'bank connect', accounting practice assessment tools, cloud computing, cyber-security hardware and software.

1.1 Once your list is complete, jot down beside each tool

   (i) The number of years each has been in use in your firm.
   (ii) The number of days or weeks it took a person to become proficient at each.
   (iii) The number of people across the firm proficient in each.

CHAPTER ONE: ACCOUNTANTS SHOULD LEARN TO JUGGLE

1.2 List the technologies your firm could adopt in the coming years? For example,

   (i) Blockchain to ensure data reliability, data security, data integrity and audit trail transparency.
   (ii) Software 'bots' to automate workflows across existing systems to aggregate data and report back.
   (iii) Deep learning and data analysis to visualise data, oversee processes, provide insight and offer guidance.
   (iv) Large Language Models, AI Apps and AGI.

1.3 Mastering a new skill takes practice and a great teacher. The better your teacher, the more you will learn.

   Make some notes regarding,

   (i) Current and emerging technologies your firm would like to investigate or master?
   (ii) Where to find the best teachers to master these emerging technologies?
   (iii) How to implement the best cyber-security solutions, policies and training? If you are unsure, please read Appendix One - Seven Bad Actors.

CHAPTER ONE: ACCOUNTANTS SHOULD LEARN TO JUGGLE

CHAPTER ONE: ACCOUNTANTS SHOULD LEARN TO JUGGLE

"At most businesses, that aren't born digital, traditional mindsets and ways of working run counter to those needed for AI."

McKinsey & Company

CHAPTER TWO
ANALYSING THE PAST

ANALYSING THE PAST

How many times have you billed a client for helping them to minimise their tax and reported profits?

As an accountant, you would not be alone.

For some accountants, diddling the tax office or shareholders out of a few dollars here and there might seem trivial. However, when this logic is permitted to grow, a firm's reputation and fees for doing so also grows. Eventually the fees grow so much that a 'Gorilla' starts hiding somewhere in the room.

An analysis of recent decades reveals that the top accounting firms have grown in gargantuan fashion. At times, these big firms have often placed profits ahead of people, the planet and ethical principles. The reason why the top four firms make up the 'Gorilla in the Room' is the often understood but curiously unspoken truth that auditor agency problems and less than arms-length dealings are still with us, usually in a disguised form.

Over the last 50 years, the concentration of expert accounting power has grown as dozens of internationally dispersed audit and accounting firms merged and then mega-merged, offering the corporate world and government departments a reduced and ethically depleted auditing choice.

CHAPTER TWO: ANALYSING THE PAST

Ethics are situational and shaped by individual preferences, values, risk profiles and needs. The small penalties for accounting fraud pose few real risks to accounting firms with limited liability partnerships, when the fees earnt for self-serving solicitous advice are so enticing.

An oligopoly is a market structure with a small number of firms, where the actions of one firm can significantly influence the others. If one firm gets away with murder, the others can be easily tempted.

In May 2005, on appeal and due to a judicial technicality, the United States Supreme Court overturned a guilty verdict of obstruction of justice against accounting firm Arthur Anderson for shredding thousands of documents and deleting emails that tied Arthur Anderson to their disgraced client, Enron.

Three years earlier, at the time of Arthur Anderson's guilty verdict, Deputy Solicitor General David Dreeben told the Court, "It is the equivalent of sending someone to a crime scene and wiping up the evidence before the police get there with the yellow tape."[22] As the Securities Exchange Commission (SEC) does not accept audits from convicted felons, its guilty verdict put Arthur Anderson out of business.

At least it appeared so.

At the time, 85,000 Arthur Anderson employees lost their jobs. Arthur Anderson had been one of the five largest audit and accounting partnerships globally.

By assisting Enron in hiding massive corporate debts and losses and exaggerating profits to investors and shareholders, Arthur Anderson left the global corporate stage. Just before the Enron collapse, Enron used EY and PwC to pressure Arthur Andersen into meeting their unethical and illegal earnings expectations. Enron would allow EY or PwC to complete accounting tasks to create the illusion of hiring a new company to replace Arthur Andersen.[23]

When Arthur Anderson failed, the stage was left to the remaining four audit and accounting partnerships. Today these top four firms: Deloitte, EY, KPMG and PwC make up the 'Gorilla in the Room' with a combined annual revenue of two hundred billion pounds (£200B).

DELOITTE

At the age of 15, William Welch Deloitte was working in London's bankruptcy courts and began learning the trade of detecting accounting fraud. In 1845, at twenty-five years of age, Deloitte established his accounting firm. Some of his early clients were shareholders in the Great Western Railway, who asked Deloitte to expose the Railway's crooked auditors and company directors. He then forced the crooked auditors and directors to resign.[24]

Deloitte was appointed to audit the Railway's books periodically, and he became the first independent professional auditor of a major company.

CHAPTER TWO: ANALYSING THE PAST

Today Deloitte, EY, KPMG and PwC audit 100% of the UK's top 100 corporations, 99% of Australia's top 200 public companies, 98% of listed companies in Germany, Italy, Spain and the Netherlands, 97% of US public companies and 80% of Japanese listed companies. In more recent times, when it came to exposing accounting fraud in large fee-paying companies, the top four have been prepared to do more than look the other way. They have actively deceived and kept quiet.

In 2007, Deloitte's silence around the Royal Bank of Scotland's falsely inflated value enabled the disastrous acquisition of the worst parts of Dutch Bank ABN Amro.[25, 26]

In 2013, Deloitte was fined US$10M for having watered down a report into how Standard Chartered Bank had hidden £250B worth of illegal transactions with Iran. [27,28]

Then again, in 2013, international short sellers exposed a string of blatant accounting frauds designed to vastly inflate profits, with one researcher linking Deloitte's China arm to seventeen known cases of accounting fraud. [29, 30]

In 2016, The Public Company Accounting Oversight Board announced a "US$8M settlement with Deloitte Brazil for violations including issuing materially false audit reports and twelve individuals were also sanctioned for various violations."[31]

By 2017, in Europe, a Deloitte partner was charged with criminal offences. Deloitte was fined €12M when a judge determined that Deloitte "showed a more than reproachable lack of attention and care" and "absolute non-observance of the rules of independence."[32] Deloitte has specialised in schemes that pushed bankers' bonuses through offshore companies from which the money would re-emerge as dividends or loans to reduce personal tax bills.[33]

Indeed, a periodic visit to the United States Department of Justice, Office of Public Affairs website reveals the most up-to-date transgressions of Deloitte and the other 'Big Four' firms. One simply needs to search 'Reuters' or 'Bloomberg' along with the name of the firm and the year to stay current with misconduct news. This search revealed that, in 2018, Deloitte agreed to a $149.5 million settlement with the U.S. government for failing to detect fraud in the audits of Taylor, Bean & Whitaker Mortgage Corp.

In 2019, Deloitte and a partner were fined for audit failures related to Serco Geografix's fraudulent activities. Deloitte faced legal action in 2021 for failing to identify irregularities in the audits of Singapore oil trader Hin Leong. In 2022, the U.S. SEC fined Deloitte's Chinese affiliate $20 million for improperly allowing clients to conduct their own audit work. By 2023, Deloitte was fined $31 million, and its Beijing operations were suspended for three months due to audit negligence.

Today, William Deloitte must be spinning in his grave.

The Deloitte arm of the 'Gorilla' is not that different from its other three limbs, as we shall see. It appears that the motivation to engage in accounting fraud from time to time is a gamble each limb is prepared to keep taking.

CHAPTER TWO: ANALYSING THE PAST

EY

Pavlovian conditioning involved ringing a bell at the same time a scientist fed a hungry dog.[33] Eventually, a trainer only needs to ring a bell to make the dog salivate. It is possible to train a gorilla or an accountant in the same way. We condition them to understand that bunches of bananas or dollars are available if they are prepared to steal them when no one is watching. The gorilla waits till the keeper is away. The accountant relies on double-entry accounting and a belief that they will not be caught.

An accountant is more cunning than a gorilla because they can accelerate their profits by also helping their clients to steal. The client pays for customised advice and a fit-for-purpose (the client's purpose) set of accounts. Each of the top four has learnt from experience. On those relatively rare occasions when the ruse is up, the client goes to jail. And the accountancy firm gets a suspension or a fine, which usually represents a fraction of the fees paid to them by the client.

In 1966, Ernst and Young (EY) were caught when their client, an investment company named Westec, raised its share price thirty-fold and tried to manipulate the stock market.[35] EY advised on a cosmetic accounting method known as 'pooling', where long-term leases from a series of mergers are used to inflate reported earnings and radically reduce the appearance of debt. Both the Chairman and President of Westec were jailed, and EY was suspended from taking on audit clients for six months.

EY's subsequent appeal in the Westec case overturned their suspension and established a precedent that has kept in-play the oligopolistic audit profession we have today. Again, forty years on, in 2005, the US Supreme Court overturned a guilty verdict of obstruction of justice against accounting firm Arthur Anderson at Enron, theoretically allowing the firm to return unfettered.

In the end, twenty-one Enron executives were jailed, however, Arthur Anderson won and was reinstated. Three years later, after the Global Financial Crisis and the collapse of Lehman Brothers, it became clear that EY had helped structure worthless CDOs, and its audit of Lehman was also worthless.[37]

With the Lehman collapse, EY Partners and employees were not jailed. The parties settled a 2010 accounting fraud lawsuit against EY for US$10M.[38] When compared to the US$150M fees Lehman paid EY between 2001 and 2008, US$10M was chicken feed! As a result of its low-quality track record, in recent years, EY rebranded itself from 'Quality in Everything We Do' to 'Building a Better Working World.'

For EY, the greatest fine imposed since 2010, was in 2022, where EY was fined $100 million by the U.S. Securities and Exchange Commission. The fine was due to EY audit professionals cheating on Certified Public Accountant (CPA) ethics exams and misleading the SEC during its investigation of the misconduct. This penalty is noted as the largest ever imposed by the SEC against an audit firm for such an issue.

CHAPTER TWO: ANALYSING THE PAST

KPMG

A friend's son recently took a graduate role with KPMG. In his first assignment, he took a trip to a regional city with his manager. Before the government client meeting, the manager advised my friend's son to lie to the client if they inquired about his positional status in the firm. The manager told this young man to say he was a senior advisor, not a graduate.

When this young man queried me about it, I did not voice my thought that it could be a simple case of misplaced professional pride on his part. My sense was that the manager's direction was unreasonable and unethical. I know it is not possible to pass judgement on a firm the size of KPMG based on the transgression of one rogue manager in a firm of 200,000 professionals. The exception does not prove the rule.

However, if this alleged incident proves to be common practice in any or all of the top four, it provides insight into a subversive if not sticky culture. It also sends a message to new recruits that the 'golden rule' is alive and well. In the good old days, the golden rule was 'do unto others as you would have them do unto you.' The new Golden Rule's ethic seems to be, 'he who counts the gold makes the rules.'

I recently reviewed the following ethical principles with a senior partner of a major accounting firm and asked which ethical principles below were most at stake within the top four firms. She replied with little hesitation, "respecting the dignity of others."

The eight ethical principles are as follows: [39]

1. Fiduciary – act in best interest of the company and investors.
2. Property – respect property and rights of those who own it.
3. Reliability – keep promises, agreements and commitments.
4. Transparency – conduct business truthfully and openly.
5. Dignity – respect the dignity of others.
6. Fairness – deal fairly with all parties.
7. Citizenship – act as responsible members of the community.
8. Responsiveness – respond to legitimate concerns of others.

When I help clients develop a strategy and assess the value it creates, I have three questions.

Firstly, is the proposed action legal?

For example, are we in breach of another's Intellectual Property (IP) and hence, do we have the freedom to continue operating this way?

Secondly, does this action contribute positively to the planet, to society and to profits?

And finally, is this action ethical?

That is, does it breach one of the eight ethical principles?

If the answer to any of the three questions is problematic, it is wise to develop an alternative strategy. If all answers pass all questions favourably, then the proposed strategy is worth considering.

CHAPTER TWO: ANALYSING THE PAST

When formulating strategy, best practice means keeping the law and the eight ethical principles in mind. As financial incentives are high, the top four accounting firms will invariably be headed up by those who are more materially than ethically motivated. Of note, less than 25% of partners in the top four are women.

Early in 2021, Bill Michael, Chairman of KPMG in the UK, was forced to step aside after 'alleged comments' were made to staff in an online meeting.[40] He was also confronted over his lack of empathy for junior KPMG employees. Two female KPMG employees revealed the Chairman was breaking the law by meeting clients for coffee during lockdown periods and that he had dismissed unconscious bias as "complete crap."[41]

In response, one angry KPMG employee retorted, "There is no such thing as unconscious bias! Are you joking? Please do your research before making such statements. Check your privilege."[42]

In response, KPMG quickly elevated two female partners to run the firm and vowed to overhaul their unpopular performance management system in a bid to calm relations with staff.

After fifty-plus years, perhaps accountability and dignity are making a comeback.

PWC

The accounting firm Price Waterhouse Coopers (PwC) completes the Gorilla.

PwC's journey started in 1861 when Coopers Brothers founded an audit and accounting firm in London.[43] One-hundred-and-twelve years later, in 1973, a transatlantic merger resulted in the formation of Coopers & Lybrand. Twenty-five years later, in 1998, Price Waterhouse Coopers completed its' mega-merger. In 1998 PwC's global revenues topped £7B. By 2001, they reached £10B.[44] Today revenues exceed £60B.

In 2002, it was revealed that PwC had broken accounting rules with 16 companies over five years.[45] In one case, PwC compromised its auditors' independence. In a second case, they encouraged a client to employ the same type of accounting trick used by WorldCom in its US$3.9B fraud. Specifically, PwC helped Pinnacle Holdings, a real estate subsidiary of Motorola, to capitalise US$8.5M of costs that should have been expensed. Of that amount, US$6.8M was earned by PwC in fees for the work.

In the 14 other cases, the SEC found that PwC acted as both an auditor and consultant to companies. PwC used a fee structure that compromised their audit team's independence.

In 2007, PwC finally agreed to pay US$229M to settle a class-action lawsuit brought by shareholders of Tyco over a multibillion-dollar accounting fraud. Tyco's CEO and CFO were found guilty of taking US$600M from

CHAPTER TWO: ANALYSING THE PAST

Tyco. They were both jailed for a decade. No wealthy PwC partners or their not-so-wealthy employees were convicted.[46]

The largest fine for PwC was $625 million by the FDIC, for not detecting fraud and phantom mortgages at the failed Colonial Bank in 2009. Reuters reports that PwC contested the fine and ultimately settled for $335 million in 2019 without admitting liability, a move that spurred significant public debate.

I am reminded of Steve Wozniak when reviewing the US$3M annual compensation for each PwC accounting partner with ten plus years of service.[47] I also note retired partners can receive twenty-five to thirty percent of the average of their three highest years of earnings as a pension – for life. This annual pension, if unfunded, is paid by current client fees and employee earnings.

An annual pension close to one million dollars probably places retired partners in the 'more money than you could ever need' category.

Despite his success, Wozniak disdains the idea of accumulating huge amounts of money.

Wozniak told *Fortune* magazine, "I didn't want to be near money because it can corrupt your values."[48] When it came to money, Wozniak did not want to be in the 'more than you could ever need' category.

When Apple Computer, the world's third wealthiest company, went public in 1980, Wozniak shared his winnings generously. He gave ten million dollars of his own stock to Apple employees.

SARBANES-OXLEY

The Sarbanes-Oxley Act was established in 2002, a year after the Enron, WorldCom and Tyco accounting failures.

Sarbanes-Oxley was enacted in corporate America to strengthen auditor independence and mitigate the effect clients could have on their auditors. Today, provisions within the act are supposed to create walls between the auditing function and other services available from accounting firms. For example, a firm that publicly audits the books should not do the company's bookkeeping, internal audits, or business valuations.

Sarbanes-Oxley was designed to address problems like inadequate oversight of accountants, lack of auditor independence, weak corporate governance procedures, stock analysts' conflict of interests, ineffective disclosure provisions and the grossly insufficient funding of the Securities and Exchange Commission (SEC). Sarbanes-Oxley helps accountants juggle the right things.

Today, thanks to Sarbanes-Oxley and advancing international oversight processes, instead of being lucrative audit and accounting firms with consulting sidelines, the top four are lucrative consultancy and legal firms with auditing sidelines.

Regulators in the UK and Europe without extensive Sarbanes-Oxley like regulations have considered breaking the top four into eight so that pure auditing and accounting can return to its century-old reliability. Under Sarbanes-Oxley rules and evolving international

CHAPTER TWO: ANALYSING THE PAST

oversight processes, audit firms are banned or restricted from providing consulting, investment advisory, banking services and designing or implementing IT systems.

In response, the top four firms' suite of services has evolved to include business restructuring, economic analysis, small medium and enterprise advisory, strategy consulting, actuarial, management consulting, forensic accounting, general legal, climate change, corporate finance, human resource consulting, corporate governance and tax accounting.

Often this suite of non-audit services makes up to 80% of each firm's revenue. For example, PwC's dwindling proportion of audit revenue is just 20%. For PwC, EY, KPMG and Deloitte, becoming Strategic Accountants, operating ethically and learning to juggle makes sense. This gives them a competitive edge and offers them a powerful hedge against the advancing AI assisted automation of accounting, reporting and compliance functions.

Having a competitive edge and a powerful hedge are two lessons growing accounting firms might do well to consider. Being this adaptable will become a core trait of high growth firms.

As the 'Gorilla' continues to grow and advise more and more corporations and governments, its increasing freedoms must be accompanied with even higher levels of inter-group and outer-group responsibility. Especially, if the reputation of the accounting profession is to survive in the face of AI and evolving digitally driven scrutiny.

CAPABILTY TWO

ETHICS AND INTEGRITY

Who are you?

What do you stand for?

Give your firm a frank and honest score, out of ten, on each of the eight ethical principles. If you are not sure, have a colleague or associate you trust rate your firm's behaviour.

1. Fiduciary – act in best interest of the company and investors.
2. Property – respect property and rights of those who own it.
3. Reliability – keep promises, agreements and commitments.
4. Transparency – conduct business truthfully and openly.
5. Dignity – respect the dignity of others.
6. Fairness – deal fairly with all parties.
7. Citizenship – act as responsible members of the community.
8. Responsiveness – respond to legitimate concerns of others.

2.1 Once you have scored your firm, jot down answers to each of these questions.
   (i) Which ethical principles does your firm perform best?
   (ii) Which ethical principles could your firm improve upon?
   (iii) Which areas are still a little grey?

CHAPTER TWO: ANALYSING THE PAST

2.2 Jot down where your firm has a unique and sustainable competitive edge over other firms?

2.3 Like the top four, how might your firm hedge itself against the advancing intelligent automation of traditional reporting and compliance functions?

2.4 As a firm's automation and AI increases, their ethics and moral character often fade.

What can you do to ensure that you strive to operate with higher and higher ethical standards and continually develop the moral character of your team?

CHAPTER TWO: ANALYSING THE PAST

CHAPTER TWO: ANALYSING THE PAST

"It's a little like wrestling a gorilla. You don't quit when you're tired - you quit when the gorilla is tired."

Robert Strauss

CHAPTER THREE
MANAGING THE PRESENT

MANAGING THE PRESENT

Walk into any business or operation and study it closely.

Can you see 'money on the ground'?

In a fast growing business, the concept of 'finding money on the ground' metaphorically highlights the loss of oversight as companies expand. Diseconomies of scale set in, leading to higher costs per unit due to inefficiencies and diminished presence of management at all operational levels. Time and money are being wasted in every moment.

Most of the time people are not present.

People tend to be more present in a group.

As groups become more collegiate and familiar, 'groupthink' occurs. Homogenous groups often think alike, take fixed positions and make costlier decisions than they would alone. This is where an accountant, as an 'out of group' advisor, can help clients stay present and make better strategic and operational decisions.

Financial accounting statements help with strategy development. On the other hand, management accounting statements are used for moment-to-moment operational decision making. Enron would have done well to engage and listen to an accountant with management accounting skills, to better oversee the day-to-day running of their business.

CHAPTER THREE: MANAGING THE PRESENT

MANAGEMENT ACCOUNTING

Instead of just analysing the past, could you use management accounting to help clients make timely non-strategic decisions?

Management accounting is not always sexy. However, there are huge savings for those who stay the course.

Management accounting can help with the restructuring of capital, timing of payments, eliminating waste, lean thinking, increasing capability and capacity, reducing work and rework, and improving profit margins. Work like this leads to operational excellence, via greater operational visibility, and helps build unique capabilities that are an ongoing source of competitive advantage.

Here are some examples.

Capital Restructuring - Accountants can help clients reduce the number of factories needed by introducing a second or third shift or by selling expensive assets and leasing them back. Firms can minimise inventory levels by tracking inventory turnover ratios, so stock needed arrives just in time (JIT). By mastering the supply side, operating with zero inventories can also be achieved.

Timing of Payments - Accountants can help clients free up large amounts of capital by raising accounts receivable turnover ratios. This can be done by changing penalty-free payment terms from 30 days to 7 days and offering discounts for payments in advance. A firm's working capital requirements can also be preserved by negotiating extended payment terms with suppliers.

Eliminating Waste - Accountants can help clients see that when the production costs for a set volume of a product or service is reduced, through the elimination of wasteful activities, the profit margin for each unit increases. Toyota Motor Corporation first embraced the ideas of economic waste and its elimination. Such Toyota Production Systems (TPS) eventually morphed into Lean Thinking, which firms then applied to functions like marketing, HR, IT and accounting.

Lean Thinking - Accountants can use lean thinking to ensure clients no longer pay for something they don't need. In the long run, firms can invest permanent savings in more strategic ways. While just the tip of the iceberg, here are some results of Lean Thinking:

- Eliminating shipping costs by not requiring defective products to be returned
- Reducing outbound logistical costs using an IKEA or 'Click and Collect' approach
- Reducing the financial complexity of cost systems, which lowers audit fees
- Auditing of all external contracts to ensure the business gets what it pays for
- Not hiring a replacement when someone resigns once a workforce improves its capacity
- Optimise run volumes to minimise expensive and time-consuming setup processes

CHAPTER THREE: MANAGING THE PRESENT

Increasing Capability - Accountants can advise clients to invest in new capabilities. Especially capabilities that align with the client's strategy. Investments fall into three categories; smart-money, dumb-money and just-money. If investing in a new capability results in returns that are valued greater than the firm's cost of capital, they are called 'smart-money' investments.

On the other hand, 'dumb-money' investments deliver returns below a firm's cost of capital. 'Just money' investments deliver returns equal to the firm's cost of capital.

Increasing Capacity - Accountants can help clients understand that when setup times are reduced, new production capacity is unlocked. Increased output from more production runs leads to increased profitability. More runs per day can result in smaller batch sizes, which in turn leads to reduced work-in-progress and finished product inventories. Reduced inventory levels free up physical space.

When space is saved, a firm can keep growing without leasing added facilities. Other space reduction examples include creating split levels within a factory, right-sizing work areas or co-locating activities to capture workflow synergies. As work areas are right-sized and workflows synergised, supervision becomes easier.

Reducing Work and Rework - Accountants can help clients realise that as supervision improves, a client can eliminate wasteful steps and minimise errors. Time and money wasted on rework are freed up, and previously lost capacity is recovered. People freed from a process, who are no longer needed, can spend more time being trained for higher-quality and value-adding work, which results in a more motivated and productive workforce.

QUALITY MANAGEMENT

Lean Thinking helps eliminate economic waste, achieve greater productivity and deliver higher quality. Lean Thinking was the result of work carried out by three quality gurus, Edward Deming, Joseph Juran and Phil Crosby.[49]

Deming demonstrated that improving product quality concurrently reduced costs. This, in turn, reduced waste production, staff turnover and litigation. Deming's cause-and-effect chain resulted in increased customer loyalty and greater profit.

Deming created the Plan-Do-Check-Act practice loop of continuous improvement, so disparate and incongruent business activities might eventually become a seamlessly integrated whole.

Like Deming, Juran's ideas took root in many Japanese corporations. Juran highlighted the importance of top management expectations of quality. Juran believed that quality management began at the highest point in the organisation and then continued to the bottom. Earlier work by Vilfredo Pareto often influenced Juran's thinking. Juran realized that 80% of an organisation's problems came from only 20% of the causes.[50]

CHAPTER THREE: MANAGING THE PRESENT

As a result, Juran coined the phrase "The Vital Few and the Trivial Many".

In his later years, Juran preferred saying "The Vital Few and the Useful Many", implying that the remaining 80% of the causes must not be ignored entirely. In his final analysis, Juran identified that the root cause of quality issues was human resistance to change and the breakdown of human relations.

Crosby's quality ideas of "Zero Defects" and "Doing it Right the First Time" were added to management thinking, along with the notion of total conformance to the customer's requirements.

Like Deming and Juran, Crosby also believed that quality management began at the highest position in the organisation and then continued to the bottom. An accountant who wants to become more valuable will do well to keep quality management issues front and centre in their dealings with clients.

At a practical level, driving a comprehensive quality management system initiative into a client organisation is not something every accountant wants to take on. However, a great deal of value can be added by adopting management accounting methods and lean thinking questions to capital restructuring, eliminating economic waste, cash flow incentives, capability investment and capacity creation.

Another enduring and highly accessible method used by strategic thinkers is the Five Whys.

FIVE WHYS

Decision making from a place of ignorance is dangerous.

Ignorance can be countered with a higher-order thinking practice such as Five Whys.

Five Whys is an interrogative technique that challenges our assumptions and explores the cause-and-effect relationships at the heart of a particular problem.[51] Knowing what is going on leads to valid assumptions. It avoids logic traps - asking why five times in an iterative fashion can radically reduce the risk of error and paint a clearer picture of the likely causes of a problem.

When clients understand the why behind the what and the how, they are motivated to innovate and change things for the better. If we ask why our executive team lacks gender diversity, the answer might be that few if any women ever apply for C-Suite roles. Then, we ask why that is. The next response might be that women candidates lack the necessary experience.

Then, we ask why that is, a total of five times.

Why? – There are never or very few women applying for C-Suite roles.
Why? – Women candidates lack management experience.
Why? – All middle managers in our firm are male.
Why? – 95% of female grads leave within 5 years.

CHAPTER THREE: MANAGING THE PRESENT

Why? – People do not leave organisations; they leave managers! (Fifth why, a possible root cause)

This series of 'why' questions can be taken further to a sixth, seventh, or higher level; however, five iterations often uncover enough of the root cause.

Using Five Whys can be helpful, but it is not foolproof.

We may recognise that the finding "People do not leave organisations, they leave managers!" is a symptom, not the real root cause.

Sometimes the lower root cause may be beyond the investigator's knowledge, and technical analysis will be necessary. In the above example, a series of exit interviews with former staff may uncover unpleasant truths about unconscious and unhealthy leadership biases within a work culture.

FIXED COSTS AREN'T

From time to time, I hear unconscious leaders use terms like fixed costs and variable costs. Instead, what I witness is a business with neither the patience, courage, nor intelligence to capture cost efficiencies. In my experience, most of the time, most companies are economically inefficient.

In the past, I would say to such clients, "Fixed costs aren't fixed. If you haven't got the patience, courage or intelligence to challenge the cost structure of your business, pay someone to do it for you."

Today, I often suggest giving the job to AI.

There are many benefits to knowing and reducing your clients' costs.

Courage, patience and intelligence are needed.

Courage means challenging cost structures, setting budgets and informing staff of the figures. Courage means being willing to impose disciplinary action on those who break the budget. Courage also means getting multiple quotes annually for all the services and products a firm uses. Eliminating waste and unnecessary purchases can be achieved by insisting staff only buy with an authorised purchase order.

Managers can inform staff that purchase orders are not personal but a way to consider if the current spending is essential.

Patience means not spending money the business will never have. Debt financing for the purchase of some assets can be a smart strategic move. Borrowing to pay for liabilities is not. Just because the banks offer more credit, that doesn't mean further loans are a good idea. When the major banks have been 'Drinking the Kool-Aid', reserve banks bail them out. The government will not bail out a business that borrows too much.

Intelligence means making sure staff purchase intelligently. Intelligence means taking stock on consignment. Intelligence means keeping 'paid for stock' at JIT levels. If there's an industry 'buying group' going, encourage clients to join it. If not, they can start one. Explore strategic sourcing by reducing the number of suppliers to capture new scale and scope economies. Understand and be ready to implement cost-saving backward-integration options when they stack up.

ACTIVITY BASED COSTING

One way to manage costs is to use Activity Based Costing (ABC), which breaks down each activity in a business and treats it separately.[52] ABC helps juggle and manage costs so that costs are something a firm can control, rather than costs controlling the firm. ABC seeks to apportion overhead costs to products on a realistic basis, based on the number and types of transactions that drive expenses across activities. ABC aims to identify which products and actions are responsible for which costs.

No costs stay the same.

As we have seen, fixed costs aren't fixed. Variable expenses are invariably super-variable. Super-variable costs sit below the gross profit line and typically increase faster than production or sales volumes. Super-variable costs include expenditure on technology, marketing, selling, distribution, innovation, product development and general administrative support for customers, channels and divisions.

The combination of advances in technology and the proper allocation of costs means some historical expenditure categories can not only be reduced, but instead, be eliminated. Previously budgeted items like stationery, filing cabinets, landline telephone systems, TV commercials and newspaper advertising can be eliminated.

This simple ABC example (in $000s) shows overall Company results along with the relative performances of Product A and Product B, with Economic Value Added (EVA) scores for each.

ITEM	COMPANY	PRODUCT A	PRODUCT B
Sales	+1000	+600	+400
Cost of Sales	-480	-240	-240
Gross Profit	**520**	**360**	**160**
Selling Expense	-210	-90	-120
Channel Expense	-116	-36	-80
Admin Expense	-108	-48	-60
Operating Profit	**86**	**186**	**-100**
Capital Costs	-100	-60	-40
EVA	**-14**	**126**	**-140**

CHAPTER THREE: MANAGING THE PRESENT

ABC analysis reveals that the overall Company loss of $14,000 is due to the lack of Product B performance. At a simplistic level, the Company might do well to discontinue Product B in favour of Product A. However, further research is needed. In the end, the Company may find that highly profitable and low-cost to serve customers buy Product A and low-profit and high-cost to serve customers buy Product B.

Future tactics might include conceding low-profit high-cost customers to competitors or re-pricing Product B upwards, based on the cost-to-serve for those who buy it. At the same time, loyalty programs and sign-on discounts could be offered to new low cost-to-serve Product A customers from the competition.

ABC can help reveal a company's low cost-to-serve customers, who:

- Order standard products and services
- Buy high quantities
- Have predictable ordering patterns
- Request standard delivery timeframes
- Make payment promptly and electronically
- Require little or no pre-sales or post-sales support

And reveal its high cost-to-serve customers, who:

- Order customised products and services
- Order small quantities
- Have unpredictable ordering patterns
- Demand customised and priority deliveries

- Fall behind with payments and pay manually
- Require large amounts of pre-sales or post-sales support

ABC systems are often not viable for smaller businesses; however, the principles of proper cost allocation and making sure each part of the business operates efficiently and effectively is a worthy and value-adding exercise for any business, as long as it is done regularly. In larger companies, operational efficiency decisions are usually made by lower task-level managers stationed on the front line.

As we move up the organisation, middle managers are responsible for implementing strategy and administering policy. At this level, decision making is often tactical. Finally, senior management must review the results from each of the lower levels and then set effective strategies, goals and policies.

In larger firms, ABC can be helpful in managing the present, so time can be freed up to create the future.

CHAPTER THREE: MANAGING THE PRESENT

CAPABILTY THREE

CRITICAL THINKING AND JUDGEMENT

How do you think?

Are you a critical thinker?

Management accounting is not always sexy. However, there are huge savings for those who stay the course and can think critically.

On the blank pages opposite, jot down some ways you could add even more value for your clients by helping them with:

1. Restructuring of capital to free up cash
2. Timing of payments to improve cash flow
3. Eliminating wasteful activity to save time and money
4. Increasing strategic capabilities
5. Improving capacity utilisation
6. Reducing unnecessary work
7. Elimination of costly rework
8. Improving profit margins

3.1 Financial performance is better in firms that have gender diversity on their Boards. Research reveals that when women are included on the Executive, return-on-equity (ROE) improves by 47% and earnings-before-interest-and-tax (EBIT) improves by 55%.[53]

On the blank pages opposite, carry out a Five Whys assessment on the following statement.

"Financial performance is better in firms that have gender diversity on their Board."

3.2 Not all clients are created equal. ABC analysis can reveal that some clients are low cost-to-serve clients and others are high cost-to-serve clients.

On the blank pages opposite, for your firm, make lists of your low cost-to-serve and high cost-to-serve clients.

3.3 List some companies that you should never have taken on as clients based on ethical grounds and what they expected you to do.

What will be a valuable set of criteria for selecting ethical clients and rejecting unethical ones?

CHAPTER THREE: MANAGING THE PRESENT

CHAPTER THREE: MANAGING THE PRESENT

"The sins of the past are revealed all the way to the bottom line."

T.J. Rogers.

CHAPTER FOUR
CREATING THE FUTURE

CREATING THE FUTURE

If you could create a future that was free of competition, would you want it?

Without competition, who would keep you on your toes?

In future, the 'autonomous accountant' and the plethora of global AI assisted accounting solutions will result in competition from anywhere, at any time, on any device.

Your ability to learn about strategy sooner than rival accounting firms may be your only sustainable competitive advantage.

If a Strategic Accountant is going to help their clients create the future, they must ensure their clients create sustainable competitive advantages. This can be done by developing a set of uniquely superior firm-specific core competencies that competitors will find difficult to imitate.

A difficult to imitate approach to strategy is Two-Sided Positioning, where firms position themselves in the space between traditional product and service offerings. Examples of Two-Sided strategies include Airbnb (hosts and guests), match.com (dating), LinkedIn (employers and employees) and Facebook (advertisers and users).

By adding a third player to a Two-Sided Position, it then becomes a Three-Sided Position. This can make for an even more tightly held set of core competencies, which competitors will find difficult to imitate. Examples

CHAPTER FOUR: CREATING THE FUTURE

of Three-Sided Positions include Uber Eats (restaurant partners, delivery partners and consumers) and Xero (clients, accountants and tax office).

Once the core competencies needed by a firm are in place, the effectiveness of the strategy needs to be measured.

Creating the future is not a set and forget process.

We need to keep score.

KEEPING SCORE

To assess its success, every strategy needs a scorecard.

The Balanced Scorecard is a popular approach and provides a four-part blueprint for the future of a business:[54]

1. *Financial.* This includes a few relevant high-level financial measures such as cash flow, sales growth, operating income, and equity return. These scores help answer the question, "How are we looking to our shareholders?"

2. *Customers.* This includes measures like sales from new products, on-time delivery, market share and customer satisfaction scores. These scores help answer the question, "What is vital to our customers and stakeholders?"

3. *Internal.* This includes business process measures like production cycle time, unit costs, yields and numbers of new product introductions. These scores help answer the question, "What must we excel at?"

4. *Innovation.* This includes learning and growth measures with scores for lead times to develop next-generation products, life cycles to product maturity, and market potential alongside competitive rivalry. These scores help answer the question, "How can we continue to improve, create value and innovate?"

CHAPTER FOUR: CREATING THE FUTURE

The Balanced Scorecard prompts managers to use the four aspects to select a small number of critical scores that report each aspect of a firm's strategic performance. Balanced Scorecards are usually unsuitable for small and medium sized enterprises (SMEs) for a variety of reasons. These include the fact the SMEs often lack the long-term strategic focus that scorecards are designed to support.

As we shall see, other forward-looking scorecards, based on the same idea, have appeared since.

A Balanced Scorecard usually contains less than twenty critical scores spread across various financial and non-financial aspects. These can be easily automated once key inputs are connected. As a result, software-driven dashboards with visual ways of displaying scores are now commonplace.

Today, these dashboards are being converted into 'bots' that run on our devices and notify us in real-time of our strategy's success or failure.

A successor to the Balanced Scorecard is the Thematic Goal Model by Patrick Lencioni.[55, 56] For those interested, Pat's model applies to the public sector as well as private sector organisations. Both scorecards urge leaders to provide a compelling context for their employees to work towards.

Scorecards are simple yet empowering tools for promoting clarity and organisational unity. As a business grows, or shrinks due to poor execution, scorecards are helpful. Scorecards can offer new ideas for maximising alignment between strategy and operational activities.

SECRETS TO GROWTH

Every business starts as an idea.

The best entrepreneurs know precisely how their idea will make money, who will buy it and why.

Entrepreneurs are adept at assembling a talented management team, know how much money will be needed and where to get it. From a strategic standpoint, entrepreneurs should articulate the new venture's unfair advantage. That is, they should anticipate how a competitor will finish the sentence, "That's not fair, your new venture has… "

When it comes to money, entrepreneurs know that investors feel a lot better about risk if the venture's end game is discussed upfront. End game discussions are supported by identifying the 'natural owner' that will ultimately acquire the business. For example, a new flavourful bottler in the soft drink market knows that if they do well, Coca Cola or Pepsi will eventually buy them out for a nice profit. Seasoned investors and venture capitalists prefer businesses that have a clear strategic focus.

Investors like companies that have a narrow focus on what the company intends to do. They also investigate whether the new venture has made plans to invest a sufficient amount of effort and money into the business. The more mature a company, the more investors look to the financials. With a newer business, the 'pitch' and the quality of the team 'on the bus' matter more than the financials.

CHAPTER FOUR: CREATING THE FUTURE

Ultimately, new business ventures can grow through six stages.[57] At each stage of growth, the needs of the business changes.

These six stages are:

1. Existence
2. Survival
3. Success
4. Take-Off
5. Maturity
6. Re-invention

An owner's ability to run the business, produce healthy cash flows and attract customers will be critical at the Existence and Survival stages. At the Success stage, the owner's ability to work in the business is still important; however, the delegation of responsibilities and having quality staff is essential. Once a business reaches the Take-Off stage, having strategic and operational plans is critical. Most companies are sold, merged or carved up at the Maturity stage. At this point the founder usually exits.

At the Re-invention stage, a mature business must learn to be entrepreneurial again and actively cannibalize itself before its competitors do. A detailed guide to the six stages of business growth appears in my previous book *The Strategy Note*.[58] When a Strategic Accountant makes it their business to understand the mix of ingredients that make up a successful venture, they can help new venture clients and their own firms to build growing and sustainable businesses.

THE STRATEGIC ACCOUNTANT

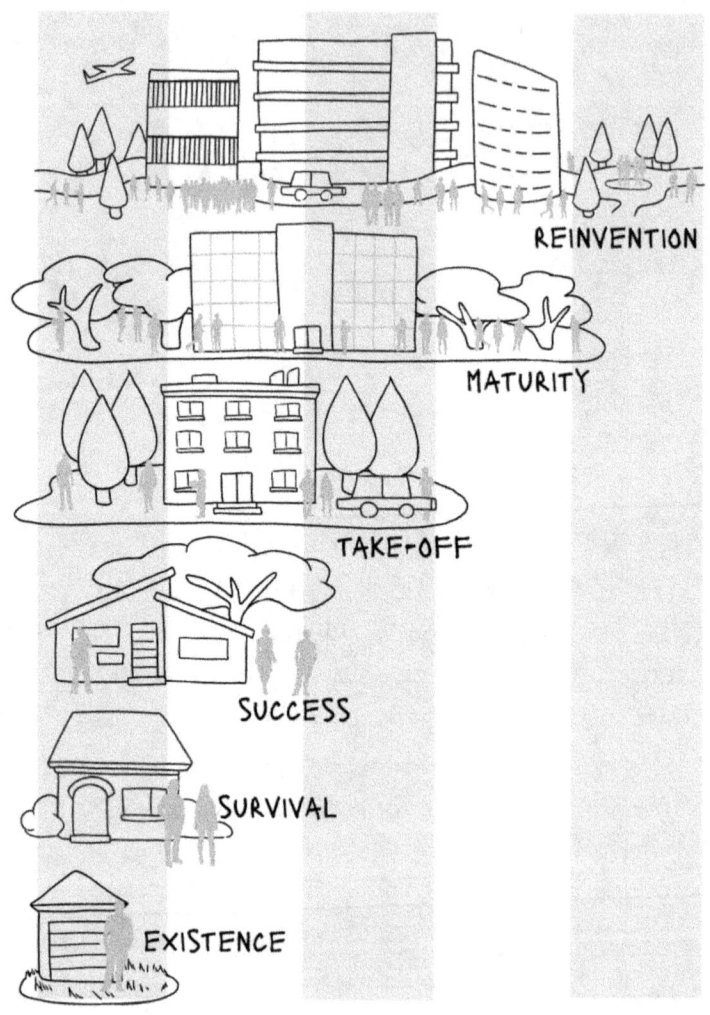

CHAPTER FOUR: CREATING THE FUTURE

PARETO EFFECTS

Growing a sustainable business is a juggling act.

Firstly, managing the present is about doing things the right way, over and over again.

Secondly, when it comes to creating the future, deciding the right things to do and the things to stop doing, are critical.

The first approach, doing something right, will make for an efficient business. The second approach, doing the right things, will make for an effective business.

In the end, managing the present efficiently might contribute to 20% of a firm's result. However, doing the right things might contribute to 80% of a firm's future, if they choose well. While more commonly referred to as the 80/20 Rule, the Pareto Principle is a powerful tool.

Joseph Ford, a notable Chaos Theorist, once said, "God plays dice with the Universe. However, they are loaded dice. And the main objective is to find out by what rules the dice are loaded with and how we can use them for our ends."[59] When applying the 80/20 Rule to create the future, we might see that less than 20% of a client's activities, products, and customers contribute to 80% of their results.

The Pareto Principle reveals that having a large and straightforward business is better than having a large and complex business. Large complex companies are more likely to fail or be carved up by a new owner. Large straightforward businesses routinely eliminate unprofitable products. They reduce their reliance on less profitable customers and markets. Large straightforward companies have the time to be ruthless with waste and refine their strategy in ways that make them uniquely different from their competition.

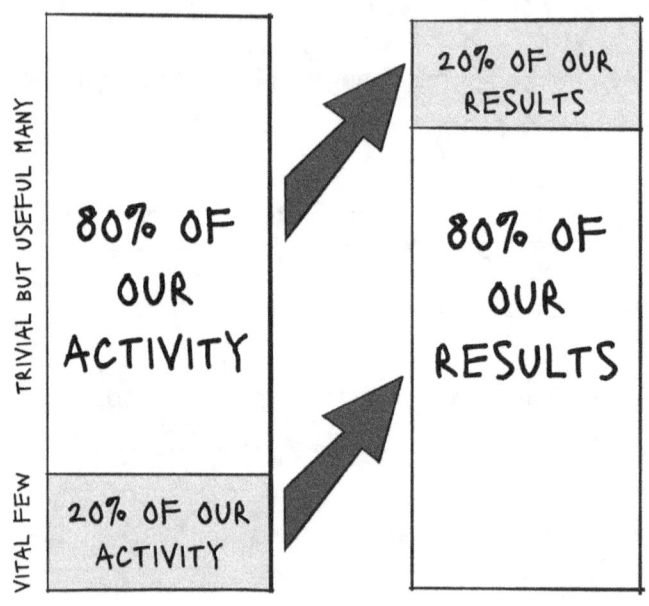

In recent years, doing the right things at Samsung and Apple has seen Apple source its unique Super Retina edge-to-edge iPhone screens from Samsung. By helping Apple with 20% of its phone componentry, Samsung retained 80% of the screen market. This stopped Apple from turning to LG, which makes screens for Google Pixel phones or Beijing Oriental Electronics Group (BOE), which makes screens for Huawei phones.

CHAPTER FOUR: CREATING THE FUTURE

With a payment from Apple of US$110 per screen, Samsung has increased its profits in two ways.[60] Apple pays on-time and for a reasonable price. By looking for 80/20 situations, a Strategic Accountant goes beyond reporting and compliance and helps create a better future for their clients, and in some cases, their client's entire industry.

SCALE

The ability to scale-up eludes companies in most industries.

To scale successfully, businesses must make trade-offs .

These trade-offs include relinquishing some or all of the founder's lofty mission-driven values in return for changes in ownership and funding to extend the business's reach. The decision to scale is sometimes forced. In some markets, the decision to scale-up allows a firm to capture an early lead, enabling it to survive.

In such "grow or die" scenarios, scale may be mandatory, whether founders like it or not.

This was the case with a client of mine named Selene.

Selene formulated a planet-friendly range of soaps and hair care products. To get her precious products to market, Selene was forced to sell 70%

of her business to a partner who provided both the manufacturing and distribution needed to scale her business. However, this entailed a change to some of Selene's product ingredients. This early need for outside capital to scale often creates tensions between a founder's values and the profit margins demanded by capital providers.

Eventually, a multi-national corporation found the capital to buy Selene and her partner out. Selene's famous planet-friendly formulations morphed into skincare and beauty products that were not as natural or planet-friendly as she would have liked. When we accept the truth of 'grow or die' scenarios, new possibilities emerge.

Like Apple and Samsung, where possible, firms should capture economies of scale to remain competitive. The more volume a firm produces, the lower its unit costs. On the supply side, the firms that get 'to scale' can demand volume discounts and favourable payment terms. On the distribution side, larger firms have the funds to buy dominant positions in sales channels, afford 'super bowl commercials' and pay supermarket shelf fees. Scale also allows firms to reduce prices to capture even more sales and win a protracted pricing war.

As businesses scale, they mustn't get "stuck in the middle". Many industries have a u-shaped relationship between their size and profitability. Prominent mass-market players like Apple can be highly profitable, often via economies of scale. Smaller niche players like Zoom can also be highly profitable, especially during pandemics. So, deciding to be much bigger or stay small are good options. An example of a firm that may be "stuck in the middle" is Tesla.

CHAPTER FOUR: CREATING THE FUTURE

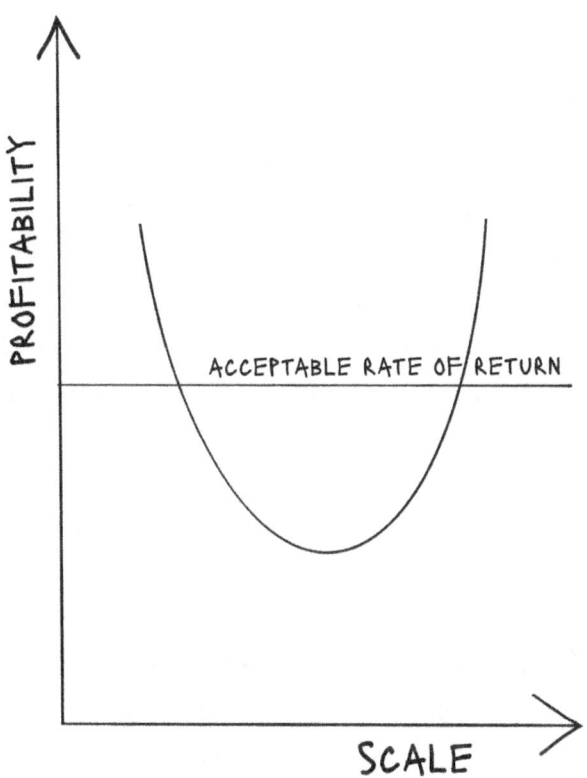

In 2020, after 18 years, Tesla recorded its first profit.

Tesla has less than 5% of the global car market and has been passed by BYD. Because Volkswagen, GM, BMW, Hyundai, BMW, and others have now entered the electric vehicle segment, Tesla must quickly "grow or die". To survive, Tesla must "right-size" itself or risk being merged with a more prominent car player.

In the car market, right-sizing for Tesla could be to scale rapidly in the hope of ultimately beating the other car companies or niching down into the luxury or sports car segments. However, hope is not a strategy.

Another option for Tesla could be to be acquired or to license their technology to a German, Korean or Japanese consortium.

Likewise, a Strategic Accountant can decide to scale their firm through a repeated series of acquisitions, not unlike the historical scaling of the top four accounting firms. Alternatively, Strategic Accountants can find a small profitable advisory niche, like forensic accounting, insolvency or business improvement services in a chosen industry, where they can learn to advise their preferred client group on juggling past, present and future, and how to 'right-size' their clients' businesses.

A counter-intuitive way to scale a business is to physically locate that business 'Right Next Door' to a competitor. This appears to be one part of Tesla's approach, by setting up significant manufacturing in China and allowing the Chinese to imitate them, resulting in China's BYD EV. Unless your firm is H&R Block or one of the top four, it is likely that 99% of people in the world have never heard of your firm. Scaling using a 'Right Next Door' strategy works, providing each competitor differentiates from the others in some way. This is why competing telco outlets in malls enjoy adjacent shop fronts.

This is why there are 41 theatres between 7th and 8th Avenues on Broadway, why furniture franchises sit alongside IKEA stores, and why all Chinese restaurants in a Chinatown precinct will enjoy a reputation that allows them to make more sales than a stand-alone Chinese restaurant.

CHAPTER FOUR: CREATING THE FUTURE

POST-STRATEGY AUDITS

Edge of Tomorrow, starring Tom Cruise and Emily Blunt, is a popular combat movie with a novel strategic theme that incorporates learning loops.[51] Major Bill Cage, played by Tom Cruise, and his airborne attack squad face daily battles against a vast alien invasion made up of an Omega and numerous Alphas. As the highest form of alien intelligence, the Omega executes her daily strategy via the Alphas. If an alien Alpha is terminated, the Omega resets the day and adjusts its tactics until the day's battle is won.

In a pivotal repeat battle, Cage uses an exploding mine to kill a significant Alpha, which covers Cage with alien blood. Accidental ingestion of alien blood allows Cage to inadvertently 'hijack' the Omega's ability to reset time. Cage resets the day's events and brings deceased Sergeant Rita Vrataski, played by Emily Blunt, back to life. Thanks to his new powers, Cage can repeat the day of the alien attack over and over.

Each day, before their next doomed attack, Vrataski and Cage can assess which of their actions against the aliens from the day prior had been effective and worthwhile.

Vrataski and Cage's 'live-die-repeat' loops allow them to keep learning. Over many loops, Vrataski trains Cage to excel in combat. With each loop, Cage becomes increasingly skilled in fighting the aliens.

The discipline of looping back and carrying out post-strategy audits is rare. Most people don't enjoy looking back at past failures. When a client avoids the learning that comes from examining failures, they 'throw the baby out with the bathwater.' The discipline of post-strategy audits is worthwhile. Comparing cash flows before and after a strategy has been implemented helps us assess the value created.

Post-strategy audits are easier to stomach than alien blood and are an excellent way to measure our intended strategy's effectiveness and evaluate whether our investment outcomes have been achieved.

Post-strategy audits also facilitate organisational learning, which includes the quality of leadership decision-making that exists. Post-strategy audits can enhance our ability to juggle the past, manage the present, and create the future.

Post-strategy audits can be facilitated using Strategy Notes. As we will see, Strategy Notes are both the endpoint and the beginning point to The Strategic Mindset Process.[62]

CHAPTER FOUR: CREATING THE FUTURE

CAPABILTY FOUR

FUTURE FOCUS

How do you grow?

Do you track and audit your firm's growth?

Post-strategy audits are needed to keep learning. To audit your strategy, you need a scorecard.

4.1 On the blank pages opposite, create a Balanced Scorecard for your firm.

Jot down some ways you could score your firm's future strategies.

(i) *Financial.* "How are we looking to our owners?" - This includes a few relevant high-level financial measures such as cash flow, sales growth, operating income and equity return.

(ii) *Clients.* "What is vital to our clients and employees?" - This includes measures such as fees from services, timeliness of work, client numbers, staff engagement levels, service standards and client satisfaction scores.

(iii) *Internal.* "What must we excel at?" - This includes business process measures such as process times, labour costs, automation improvements and numbers of hours billed.

(iv) *Innovation.* "How can we continue to improve, create value and innovate?" - This includes learning and growth measures, new value adding services, rates of AI adoption and performance relative to the competition.

4.2 Identify which Stage of Business Growth your firm has reached. If you are unsure, please re-read the section on Secrets to Growth.

1. Existence
2. Survival
3. Success
4. Take-Off
5. Maturity
6. Re-invention

4.3 Is your firm small, medium-sized or large?

Small and large firms are often highly profitable. Medium-sized firms usually have more significant challenges. Medium-sized firms often scale via a series of mergers and acquisitions to capture synergies which align with their longer-term goals.

Which way would you like your firm to grow?

How will you measure it?

CHAPTER FOUR: CREATING THE FUTURE

CHAPTER FOUR: CREATING THE FUTURE

*"Imagine entering the cockpit of a modern jet airplane
and seeing only a single instrument there."*

Robert S. Kaplan

CHAPTER FIVE
CULTIVATING A STRATEGIC MINDSET

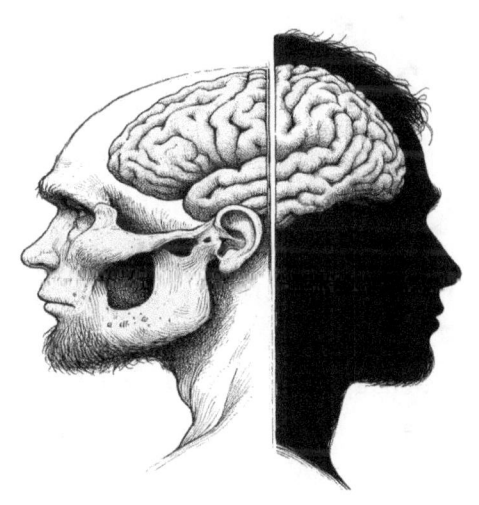

CULTIVATING A STRATEGIC MINDSET

Which brain would you prefer?

A Neanderthal brain or the one you were born with?

During my conference talks on strategy, I produce a life-sized replica of a Neanderthal skull and introduce audiences to 'my old mate Fred.' I then share why Neanderthals were eliminated. Scientists have found that fifty-thousand years ago, after the last ice age, as flora and fauna returned sporadically, food became scarce. At that time, our hungry Homo-Sapien ancestors scaled the Italian Alps to a vista of breath-taking snowy mountains and ultimately conquered Fred's species. Fred and his kinsfolk appear to have been eradicated by tribes of Sapiens heading north and spreading across the Globe.

The success of the Sapiens and the failure of the Neanderthals offer valuable lessons which we can apply to the competitive and co-operative world of business. As suggested by the shape of their skulls, the Sapiens' brains differ from the brains of the Neanderthals. A Neanderthal skull is elongated and flat, like an NRL or NFL football.

Like a basketball, a Sapiens skull is rounder, shorter from front to back, with a higher and more prominent forehead. This difference means that proportionally, Fred had more room in the rear of his skull, and less room for his midbrain. Fred's small forehead meant that he had even less room for his frontal cortexes.

CHAPTER FIVE: CULTIVATING A STRATEGIC MINDSET

Some scientists suggest Fred's large rear-brain offered him excellent night vision and a heightened sensitivity to changes in his immediate environment.[63] Thanks to his larger parietal and occipital lobes, located in the rear of his skull, Fred's ability to sense and see was probably superior to ours. When southern tribes of Sapiens invaded, it is likely that Fred saw and felt their presence first. This ability to sense and see is helpful in life and business. Sensing and Seeing are the first two steps of the six-step Strategic Mindset Process.

By contrast, it is possible that Fred's smaller frontal cortex and smaller midbrain placed him at a disadvantage once we Sapiens spotted him. With larger forebrains, our ability to process information, connect and plan may have been superior. If this is true, we could have coordinated our efforts and planned our attacks with greater ease and success than Fred.

Connecting and Planning are the third and fourth steps of the six-step Strategic Mindset Process. Finally, if our midbrains were more prominent, this would have allowed us to focus and move more strategically and efficiently in the world due to our enhanced coordination, balance and motivation. At night-time, Fred could survive better, but when day broke, Fred was easy prey.

When compared with Fred, our ability to focus and move strategically is something we did better. Focusing and Moving are the fifth and sixth steps of the Strategic Mindset Process. In the end, Fred's brain probably let him down. He could sense and see well, but he may not have been able to connect, plan, focus and move fast enough. To survive and thrive in business, one must be proficient in all six steps.

To apply the Strategic Mindset Process, follow these six steps:[64]

Step 1. Sense the Environment
Step 2. See Beyond the Next Horizon
Step 3. Connect with Customers and Stakeholders
Step 4. Plan Future Value Chains, Creations and Combinations
Step 5. Focus on a Chosen Target
Step 6. Move Faster with Influence

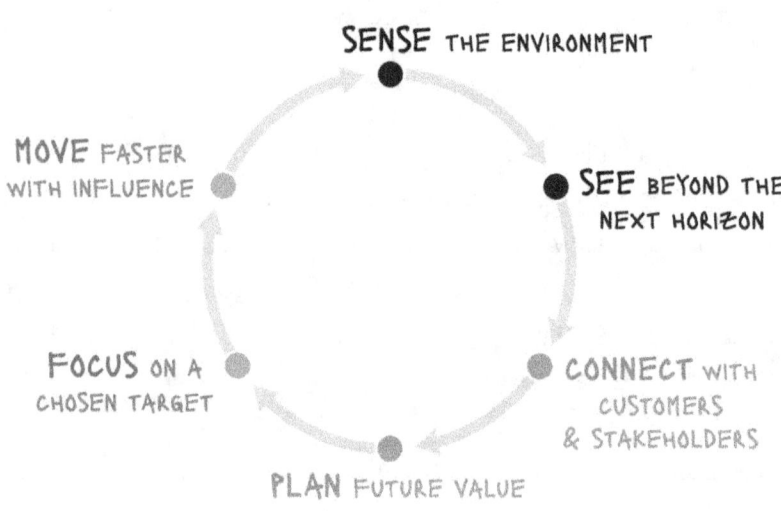

CHAPTER FIVE: CULTIVATING A STRATEGIC MINDSET

The six-step Strategic Mindset Process is straight forward and has been crystallized over many years of studying numerous industries and assisting countless businesses. The best way to master the Strategic Mindset Process is to obtain a copy of The Strategy Book.

However, in this chapter, I will share a few concepts from The Strategy Book that are a useful starting point for accountants who want to become Strategic Accountants. Becoming strategic means helping your clients compete profitably in the industries of the future.

INDUSTRY ANALYSIS

Neanderthals may not have given much thought to who their future competitors would be. Sapiens proved superior *Substitutes* to Neanderthals. Until the aliens invaded earth, Major Cage was blissfully unaware of the skills needed to deal with the *Threat of New Entrants,* like the Omega.

In 2007, as the leading mobile phone player, an ill-equipped Nokia felt like an alien force had landed when the first iPhone arrived. Twenty years ago, the world's major hotels and airlines had no idea how much their customers' *Buyer Bargaining Power* would increase with the introduction of intermediaries like Priceline, Wotif, Expedia, Trip Advisor, Booking.com and AirBNB.

At the same time, local suppliers of steel, cotton, textiles, hardware and electronics experienced increased *Rivalry* among existing firms when Chinese manufacturers entered. Local manufacturers might have changed their strategy sooner, if they'd known how quickly their *Supplier Bargaining Power* would be further eroded by global trading giants like Alibaba. Alibaba introduced a plethora of new competitors to tens of thousands of marketplaces.

Competitors can be great teachers. Competitors can drive a business to better position itself within the industries of the future. In the long run, changes in five competitive forces determine the profitability of every industry.[65] Successful firms routinely update their understanding of the rivalry among existing industry firms, buyer and supplier bargaining power, the threat of new entrants, and the threat of substitute products or services.

Furthermore, a well-positioned firm can earn above industry average returns on capital, even when the industry itself offers only average profitability.

Complements are a sixth industry-related force worth considering. This involves looking at adjacent industries. Complementary players are firms in adjacent industries with activities that complement your industry. Accountants and lawyers, whilst operating in different professions, are able to complement one another's activities via referrals.

Some industries are attractive. For example, at the time of writing, dentists enjoy 20% profit margins. For dentists, customer power, the threat of substitutes, the threat of new entrants and the degree of rivalry are low, with supplier power being high and benefits from complementary players being moderate.

CHAPTER FIVE: CULTIVATING A STRATEGIC MINDSET

CUSTOMER BARGAINING POWER 　　SUPPLIER BARGAINING POWER

THREAT OF NEW ENTRANTS 　　THREAT OF SUBSTITUTES

DEGREE OF RIVALRY 　　BENEFITS FROM COMPLEMENTS

OVERALL INDUSTRY ATTRACTIVENESS

Other industries are less attractive. For example, airlines have profit margins of just 5% with plenty of crosswinds. Usually, for airlines, supplier power, customer power, threat of substitutes, threat of new entrants and degree of rivalry are all moderate or high, with benefits from complementary players being only moderate. In the global pandemic, airline profits evaporated.

Unlike dentists, in recent years, many accountants have been able to increase profit margins to 30% using advanced software tools. For accountants prepared to automate, threats become lower from substitutes, new entrants and rivals. They may also enjoy more power over suppliers and the benefits from complementary players are higher.

COST LEADERSHIP

Good strategy involves taking a unique stance or position.

Three classic strategy positions are Cost Leadership, Differentiation and Focus.[66]

Cost Leadership means meeting the broad needs of many customers in a select market. Enron Energy sold energy to millions of users. Enron Energy became a highly profitable cost leader in the energy market by selling long-term oil, gas and electricity contracts for future supply at reduced prices when paid upfront. This long-term consumer lock-in

CHAPTER FIVE: CULTIVATING A STRATEGIC MINDSET

stance offered Enron a powerful fit when negotiating significantly reduced supply prices with energy producers.

Alas, all the pre-paid income Enron received was not invested wisely. The billions of dollars on hand appears to have been traded foolishly or quickly spent on opulent offices, countless lavish executive perks, international junkets, ski resort holidays and expensive jewellery for secretaries and PAs.

H&R Block is an example of a cost leader in the accounting space, serving the tax, financial planning, superannuation, accounting and payroll needs of millions of clients in North America and Australia.

Of the three classic strategy positions, Cost Leadership is perhaps the easiest to understand. Successful long-time investors like Warren Buffett and Charlie Munger preferred to invest in firms that adopted a cost-driven approach. Despite Enron pursuing a cost-driven approach, Buffet and Munger did not invest in Enron because the culture was toxic, and its accounting numbers did not add up. The Enron debacle echoes many of the corporate trends that Buffett warned us against.

Buffet referred to Enron as "The symbol for shareholder abuse", and Munger remarked that "Enron is certainly the most disgusting example of a business culture gone wrong."[67] In an era where aggressive accounting stunts had become widespread among corporations, Munger went on to caution accountants, "Maybe you should be extraordinarily careful if you're a partnership, in whom you take on as a client, and what you agree to."[68]

Every accountant, strategic or otherwise, should take Munger's advice. In days gone by, to justify a nice fee, many accountants manipulated figures that falsified book values instead of advising clients on strategies that added real customer and shareholder value. Buffet's long term investment portfolio was always packed with low-cost producers. Low-cost producers find and leverage multiple sources of cost advantage and sell standard products or 'basics' with little or no-frills.

Cost leaders are the best low-cost producers and charge prices at or near the industry average. A classic cost leader is Walmart, which used a Cost Leadership strategy to become the world's largest company. Cost leaders enjoy higher returns than their competitors due to their superior position as *the* cost leader.

When multiple firms are vying for the cost leader position, the resultant rivalry among these firms can be brutal. In a protracted battle, where no one firm can pre-emptively convince competing players to give up, industry-wide profitability and firm reputations can deteriorate irreversibly.

DIFFERENTIATION

Differentiation means meeting the broad needs of a select group of customers. Deloitte, EY, KPMG and PwC offer a wide range of services to the top few hundred corporations. These four firms differentiate themselves from other accounting firms by charging high fees that

CHAPTER FIVE: CULTIVATING A STRATEGIC MINDSET

signal quality advice. Their pricing stance provides a good 'fit' with their significant ability to provide high-value solutions to a select set of corporate problems.

When a firm seeks to be unique in terms of added customer value relative to other firms, it is rewarded with a price premium. Where and how to differentiate is always industry-specific and is ultimately driven by customer needs and desires. The goal is to attract a price premium that exceeds the additional costs in providing a unique product or service.

The company Whole Foods differentiates itself by going beyond just selling groceries. They understand the needs of the customer and the planet better than their competitors. They were the first to eliminate plastic bags fifteen years ago. Their cheerful store designs are as easy to navigate as their unique website. They distribute to local-only stores, avoid big chains, and partner with quality chefs to promote their food.

From time to time, I hear inexperienced and strategically challenged entrepreneurs and small business owners talking about a need to diversify their business. When I probe further, I realise that when they say diversify, they mean differentiate. While Cost Leadership is easy to understand, it takes preparedness, patience, skill, courage and luck to achieve. For this reason, most firms look to some form of Differentiation to come up with a unique selling proposition and a profitable return.

Over the last fifty years, the number of firms competing for customers has skyrocketed. This increasing concentration of players in many industries has created a much harsher competitive environment, with greater industry unpredictability and even more delinquent customers, who shop around and readily switch services, products and brands.

As a result, the modern firm must continuously find new ways to differentiate, remain relevant, safeguard market share and stay profitable. Where a less educated accountant might report on a loss of sales and then suggest a business diversifies, a Strategic Accountant proactively challenges their clients to remain focussed on their 'claim to fame' and to keep looking for unique customer-driven ways to differentiate, both now and in the future.

FOCUS

Focus means meeting the select needs for a chosen group of customers. Peat, Marwick, Mitchell & Co offered an audit only service to many firms. They focussed on being an independent public auditor and not offering other services. This stance provided a great 'fit' between its forensic style accounting expertise and its desire for integrity.

Focus is the third classic strategy position and differs from Cost Leadership and Differentiation in a simple but powerful way. Focus requires a firm to narrow its scope competitively. Focus requires the firm to exclude the lion's share of its industry and tailor its offering to a select few in a chosen segment. Examples might be an exclusive government defence contractor like Lockheed Martin, with 120,000

CHAPTER FIVE: CULTIVATING A STRATEGIC MINDSET

employees, or a heating ventilation air-conditioning (HVAC) company of 20 employees that turns over US$10M a year with only one client.

With the HVAC firm, the client could be a property management firm that manages hundreds of commercial properties. Each generic strategy, Cost Leadership, Differentiation and Focus, has its advantages and downsides. The HVAC company needs very little investment and does not require a sales force or even a website. However, if they lost their client, they could be out of business in a heartbeat.

By tailoring its operations to a particular segment or client, a Focus positioned firm gains specific knowledge about its target, offering that focussed firm a competitive advantage. This segment-specific knowledge allows a Focus positioned firm to choose either a Cost-Focused approach or a Differentiation-Focused approach.

A Cost-Focused approach is where a firm aims to be a low-cost producer or cost leader in its chosen segment. A Cost-Focused firm does not necessarily charge the lowest prices in its industry. However, it charges low prices relative to other firms that compete within the same target market. A classic Cost-Focused example is Southwest Airlines, which only competes on select regional routes with a rapid boarding no-frills service.

A Differentiation-Focussed approach occurs when the firm aims to be uniquely different in its chosen segment. A Differentiation-Focussed firm offers unique features that fulfil the demands of a narrow market. Many firms use this approach to concentrate their efforts on a particular sales channel, like the internet. Other firms target wealthy demographic groups. Ritz-Carlton is a good example, with only 100 hotels globally.

		COMPETITIVE ADVANTAGE	
		LOWER COST	DIFFERENTIATION
COMPETITIVE SCOPE	BROAD	COST LEADERSHIP	DIFFERENTIATION
		STUCK IN THE MIDDLE	
	NARROW	COST FOCUS	DIFFERENTIATION FOCUS

Ritz-Carlton amplifies the luxury of travel with breathtaking properties, fine dining and unique guest experiences, including twice-daily housekeeping, a personal concierge, complimentary food and beverage buffets and free location-specific souvenirs.

The Cost-Focussed approach and the Differentiation-Focussed approach are the two types of Focus positioning possible. A focused approach can result in a less contested market space, a richer understanding of the customer, and a more prosperous return.

CHAPTER FIVE: CULTIVATING A STRATEGIC MINDSET

RIGHT-SIZING

Right-Sizing is about creating valuable returns in unique and sustainable ways. Firms can drive value by lowering costs, being different from other players or focussing on a narrow market segment. Where a firm competes to be the best player in a crowded market, this invites imitation. Alternatively, striving to be singularly unique delays imitation. Being unique is unlikely to make the competition irrelevant; it just buys a firm additional time.

In 2002, Tesla created a singularly unique emission-free electric car. Last year, with its first accounting profit, Tesla is now capturing the value its millions of stockholders have so long-awaited. Being uniquely valuable relative to other car manufacturers bought Tesla a great deal of time. As BYD, GM, Volkswagen, Hyundai, BMW, Audi and now Ford introduce electric cars, Tesla will need to adjust its approach and right-size. As its uniqueness as a car maker fades, Tesla will need to choose between Cost Leadership, Differentiation or Focus, or a uniquely valuable combination of the three generic approaches while ensuring it does not get "stuck in the middle."

Tesla appears to be racing to scale its electric car manufacturing to reduce the risk of its car business being swallowed up by established auto giants. Scaling-up is expensive and takes time. Tesla's combined strategy of differentiation and low-cost means they may fail at both.[69] They could lose by refusing to choose. First movers often underestimate the possibility of imitation by another player, who then exposes the first mover as neither low-cost nor differentiated.

Regardless of its market share, every firm should innovate, where the cost of doing so is not expensive or prohibitive. All firms, regardless of their uniqueness, should seek cost reductions that do not compromise their differentiation. Once a firm decides on a uniquely valuable strategy, it must align its various activities with it.

A Strategic Accountant can help a client align strategy with activity by right-sizing the client's value chain. The value chain is the name given to the sequence of value-creating activities that a firm performs to create and capture value. Most value chains include inbound logistics, operations, outbound logistics, marketing and sales and customer service.[70] The way a firm performs each activity in a value chain determines the degree of economic value the chain creates for that firm.

Once a firm's strategy is known, the firm must configure its value chain to deliver on the strategy. Value chain integration options that support the three strategic generic approaches include backward integration, forward integration and horizontal integration. If you are interested, *The Strategy Book* contains an entire chapter on configuring value chains and value combinations.

However, I will share an example of each to show how value chain integration strategies work.

Backward Integration, whilst generally ill-advised, is a movement towards the supply side of the business. It can be a worthwhile move if there is a quality issue with sourced inputs. Apple started outsourcing its hardware chips from Motorola. This proved costly. Then, it backward integrated unprofitably into making chips. Then, it gave up and sourced

CHAPTER FIVE: CULTIVATING A STRATEGIC MINDSET

chips from Intel. Eventually, Intel's chips increased costs and slowed performance.

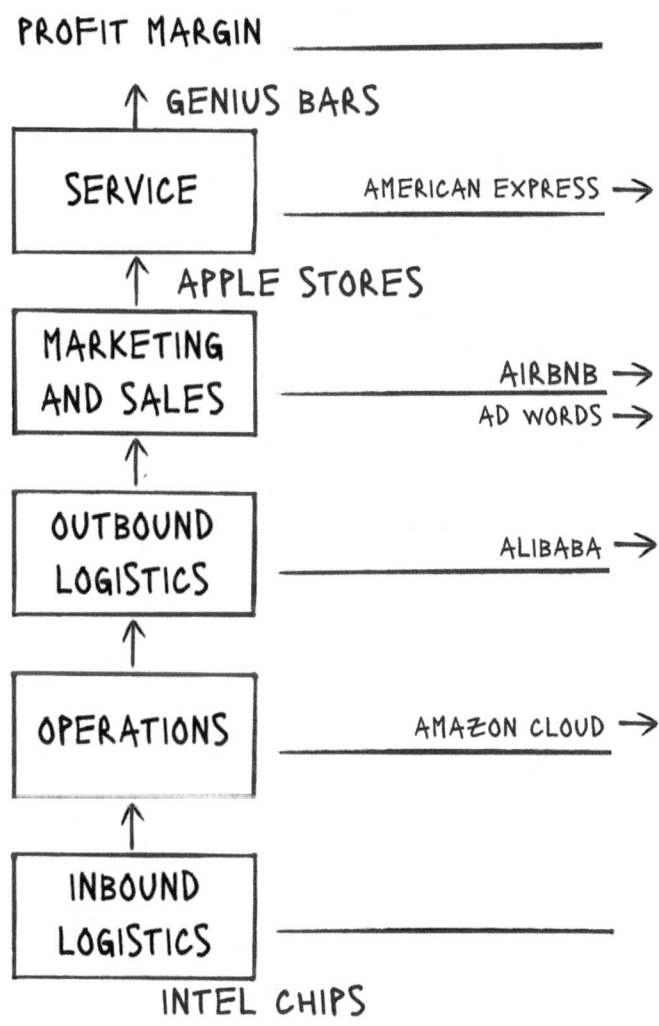

Today Apple have backward integrated once again and are making chips to save money and enhance performance.

Forward Integration is often desirable because it moves the business closer to the customer. In the early 2000s, Apple dismantled its problematic worldwide dealer network and forward integrated with customer-friendly Apple Stores and Genius Bars.

Horizontal Integration means focussing on one part of the industry value chain and promoting it on a large scale. This integration move usually enjoys positive cost and positive value drivers. Horizontal integration often uses a Two-Sided Strategy. Airbnb does this at the sales point of the value chain. UPS and Alibaba do this with inbound and outbound logistics respectively. Amazon cloud services do this with operations. Google AdWords and Facebook do this with marketing and American Express does this with customer service.

Strategic Accountants who understand the importance of industry analysis and when to use strategic approaches like Cost Leadership, Differentiation and Focus, can help right-size their firm and support their clients in configuring value chains to compete successfully and profitably in the industries of the future.

A profitable strategic approach used historically by the top four accounting firms and more actively pursued these days by mid-tier networked accounting firms like BDO are mergers and acquisitions. If this is something your firm is interested in pursuing, please read Appendix Two - Successful Mergers & Acquisitions.

CHAPTER FIVE: CULTIVATING A STRATEGIC MINDSET

CAPABILTY FIVE

STRATEGIC MINDSET

How well do you sense your environment and adapt to the future?

Unless you have a Neanderthal-like brain, sensing and seeing will be something you will have to keep training for. It's heavy work. However, once you have a clear picture of your industry and the major trends out there, it may be time to weigh up your strategic options.

5.1 Which strategic approaches or combinations of approaches make sense?

  (i) Cost Leadership
  (ii) Differentiation
  (iii) Cost Focus
  (iv) Differentiation Focus
  (v) Two-Sided or Three-Sided Positioning
  (vi) Right Next-Door Positioning

5.2 How could your firm forward integrate towards your clients to offer more reliable and valuable services?

5.3 Could your firm horizontally integrate in some way?

   For example, develop 'bots' that automate workflows across systems. Then license the 'bot' to other firms.

CHAPTER FIVE: CULTIVATING A STRATEGIC MINDSET

CHAPTER FIVE: CULTIVATING A STRATEGIC MINDSET

"Stand back, Barney. I'm going to put a little weight behind it."

Fred Flintstone

CHAPTER SIX
LEADING STRATEGY

LEADING STRATEGY

If you had to share a ten-year bus trip with ten people, who would be on the bus?

Are any of them people you work with?

Why?

Why?

Why?

Why?

Why?

A pre-requisite to a successful strategy is having the right leaders on the bus and in the right seats.

On the other hand, doomed strategies are found within dusty bound reports inside executive bookcases.

Let me explain.

CHAPTER SIX: LEADING STRATEGY

LEADING THE CITY

Early in my consulting career, I called on the CEO of a city council that became one of my clients for over a decade. In that first meeting, I asked the CEO whether the city had a strategic plan. The CEO laughed and pointed to a bound fifty-page document sitting in a nearby bookcase. The CEO explained that the Strategic Plan was out of date and 'legless' due to the lack of accountability in his workforce of over 500 employees.

As I probed further, it became clear that it did not matter what was contained in the Strategic Plan. The City Council wouldn't execute anything of lasting value any time soon. Instead of allowing me to help the city design its strategic future, the CEO invited me to teach his executive and middle management team about specific, measurable, achievable, realistic, relevant and time-based (SMAR^{2}T) goals. The process took three years!

This added accountability made a big difference in the effectiveness of public money being spent. However, a small number of executives resented the new responsibility required, and the CEO was forced out. A fortnight later, the HR Director called on me to advise on a new CEO recruitment process. After the new CEO appointment, I worked with the HR Director and the new CEO to measure the organisational culture. This helped raise awareness of conflicts and dilemmas within the City Council that contributed to its poor performance.

As the culture healed, I carried out a series of community and key stakeholder group consultations to prioritise the wider community's needs and aspirations. This allowed the rightful beneficiaries of the City's services to help guide the decision-making process. All successful firms should look to their people and customers when making strategic decisions. Likewise, an accountant can ask their clients what services would be most helpful to them and then use that feedback to become more strategic.

Back at the Council, my next assignment was Strategic Planning Facilitation, which I had first offered the City six years earlier. After the Strategic Planning was completed, the CEO then asked me to assist with the last thorny piece of the puzzle. He needed help in getting the lazy, entrenched old male guard out and new blood onto the bus. Finally, seven years later, the City's activities began to reflect the Strategic Plan. We continued to align the strategy with the needs of the City's rate-paying customers.

The expensive lesson learnt was that for Strategic Planning to become a valuable exercise, organisations must first get the wrong people off the bus and the right people on the bus and in the right seats. The other expensive lesson for the City was that the new CEO did not take my advice to move AU$40M of the City's cash reserves out of investment bank, Lehman Brothers. Three months after that, Lehman Brothers collapsed.

At that time, the CEO told me he was taking the City's Financial Advisor's advice, which was not to worry about Lehman Brothers. I shared that the CEO would have to raise ratepayer taxes if Lehman Brothers failed. Lehman Brothers failed, and the City lost its savings. It turned out the Financial Advisor was receiving trailing commissions

CHAPTER SIX: LEADING STRATEGY

from Lehman Brothers for keeping the City's money invested. With depleted cash reserves, the City could no longer afford my consulting fees, and the CEO headed off to a series of ratepayer meetings to raise taxes.

The City's Financial Advisor was not independent and was another wrong leader to have on the bus.

CULTURE EATS STRATEGY

Many years ago, as an MBA student, I was given the role of introducing corporate CEO speakers to my business school classmates. It was exciting to hear straight from the "horse's mouth" the triumphs, trials, and tribulations that existed in C-Suite teams. One CEO who spoke to us was Dennis Eck, a former supermarket management consultant. Dennis shared that he was quizzed by Coles Myer's Chairman and asked if the Strategic Plan he had just written for them was implementable. When Dennis replied, 'yes', the Board invited him to be the next CEO of Coles Myer.

Dennis shared with us that on his first day as Coles Myer CEO, he asked his Executive Assistant to remove the Values and Vision plaque on his desk and have the maintenance department hang it in the far corner of his office. When Dennis's C-Suite team arrived later that day and inquired about the plaque's whereabouts, he told his team that when they and the organisation embodied the stated Values and Vision of Coles Myer, he'd move the plaque back.

Dennis understood that fixing the senior management team's mindset and the organisational culture was the first step in transforming Coles Myer. Over the next four years, by addressing the dysfunctions in the culture, Coles' Department Store and Supermarket Groups doubled their respective market shares and, for the first time, posed a real challenge to the previously dominant Woolworths.

There is a famous saying, "Culture Eats Strategy for Breakfast." How, as an accountant, might you help your clients shift their cultural needle in a positive direction? I often share with clients the three biggest cultural mistakes businesses can make.

The third biggest mistake is not hiring the right people for the job.

The second biggest mistake is holding onto the wrong people too long.

However, the biggest mistake of all is not bringing your people together as a functional team.

There is often an opportunity for an accountant to not only account for what has taken place but, as a trusted advisor, hold their clients to account. This could be as straight forward as asking a client what areas of the business they would like to prioritise and be held accountable for.

Getting an engaged and functional team was the priority Dennis had at Coles Myer. I learnt the same lesson with the City Council CEO and

CHAPTER SIX: LEADING STRATEGY

his team. A Strategic Accountant understands that a firm's success or failure relies on both its strategy and its culture.

FIVE DYSFUNCTIONS

In an earlier chapter, I mentioned Pat Lencioni's Thematic Goal Model. Before developing this model and later leadership development tools, Pat's first framework was the *The Five Dysfunctions of a Team*.[71] If you are already committed to becoming a Strategic Accountant, pick-up a copy of Pat's book, *Five Dysfunctions of a Team*. In the book, you will discover a pyramid made up of five levels that build powerfully on one another.

Dysfunction #1: Absence of Trust
The fear of being vulnerable prevents team members from building trust with each other.

Dysfunction #2: Fear of Conflict
The desire to preserve artificial harmony stifles productive ideological conflict within the team.

Dysfunction #3: Lack of Commitment
The lack of clarity and buy-in prevents team members from making decisions they stick to.

Dysfunction #4: Avoidance of Accountability

The need to avoid interpersonal discomfort prevents team members from holding each other accountable for their behaviours and performance.

Dysfunction #5: Inattention to Results
The pursuit of individual goals and personal status erodes the team's focus on collective success.

In organisational cultures without vulnerability-based trust and a fear of conflict, strategic planning is a waste of time. However, once team members are prepared to be vulnerable with one another and feel safe enough to engage in constructive conflict around world views, unpopular topics and difficult ideas, strategic planning can provide the clarity needed to gain commitment. The team then holds

CHAPTER SIX: LEADING STRATEGY

one another accountable for those commitments and they strive towards shared results that reflect the agreed strategy.

In traditional law firms, accounting partnerships, and rigid company hierarchies with divisional silos, it is often hard to get past the third level on the pyramid. Teams in these businesses should learn to trust each other, engage in constructive conflict and gain commitment. However, many staff reporting processes actually work against accountability and collective success, typically due to partnership fiscal reward structures and the authoritarian nature of such business units or siloed partnerships. In such situations, the tendency to put their unit's success over the total firm's success is often entrenched.

To overcome such barriers, teaching all staff about higher order thinking and empowering them to challenge the status quo works best, where everyone is more interested in the client's success than their billing revenue. Firmwide commitment to Five Whys thinking and Quality Management principles encourages innovation, initiative, accountability and can result in a functional culture focussed on collective success.[72]

Could you encourage your client to get the wrong people off the bus, get the right people on board and in the right seats and then bring employees together as a high functioning team?

Ultimately, businesses need to create cultures that can cope with and manage change.

If you are able to help a client achieve this, the next step might be to help your client take their people on a learning journey around leading strategy.

LEADING STRATEGY

Three years after introducing Dennis Eck to my business school classmates and a year after commencing my journey with the City Council, I was sitting in the office of my friend Bob McInnes, a chartered accountant. Bob wanted to introduce me to his client Selene, who I mentioned previously in Chapter Four. Selene was a pro-planet advocate and chemist who, unfortunately, was broke. Instead of suggesting insolvency, Bob felt I could save her business with the right strategy.

Bob had great accounting knowledge but was not yet confident enough when it came to the right strategic approach for turning Selene's business around.

As I listened to Selene, she described her despair.

"Screw it. Nothing works. No one will buy my idea. Nobody cares for this toxic planet."

Bob spoke nervously, "Selene, maybe John can help."

CHAPTER SIX: LEADING STRATEGY

Selene groaned, "I doubt it."

My eyes widened. I let Selene's remark dissolve on my next exhale.

Selene was burdened by debt and a custody battle.

As Selene felt safer, her weary eyes released tears.

The antique clock in Bob's office chimed. Selene pulled herself together.

I encouraged Selene, "If I could grant you anything you want, what would it be?"

The blood returned to Selene's face. Selene revealed her business idea. She wanted to formulate, make and sell a range of all-natural, environmentally friendly and allergy-proof personal care products.

To grow her business, Selene needed real courage. She also needed a plan.

Two days later, I sent Selene a one-page strategy note. My note gave her an action plan she could follow as she moved forward. I was unsure whether she could avoid bankruptcy. Nevertheless, Selene now had a strategy note. A single page containing a pragmatic assessment, an overview of options, a recommendation for growing her business and three action steps.

Five years later, Selene contacted me. I was curious to hear how she was doing. Had she found the courage to grow her business? I wanted to understand if the strategy note had helped.

Selene testified that the strategy note gave her business clear options. These options were invaluable in leading her company to take brave decisions and actions. She revealed that her company was the leader in its field and had just won the state-wide business award as the best business in its category.

Then I asked Selene, "How are you feeling?"

Selene said, "People really do care about the planet and my ideas!"

I winked at Selene, "Nothing works."

Selene laughed, "True. But your strategy note did."

All those years ago, Selene, like Greta Thunberg, might have labelled the pandemic and global warning as an omen or even retribution. Whatever the cause, the current climate dilemma is 'the perfect storm' for businesses worldwide.

The challenge for advisors is to find ways to help their clients re-build their businesses in sustainable ways. As a Strategic Accountant, you can help clients do this by cultivating the discipline of a one-page strategy note.

CHAPTER SIX: LEADING STRATEGY

A strategy note is a time-limited one-pager that sheds light on strategy and communicates the actions needed. A one-page strategy note reflects the understanding that crafting strategy in ways that do not harm the planet and aligning people with strategy, are the crowning aspects of leadership. Indeed, the most effective strategic plans do not contain fifty-pages of analysis and industry references, which no board member, manager or employee wants to read.

Strategy and recommendations are best understood in person.

When it is not possible for a leader to share strategy in person, they must use another form of communication. Strategic Accountants can help their clients create a script to be shared in people's presence or absence. This script is best communicated on a single page and in a format that reliably informs the reader of the strategic intent and the actions needed.

As a client's business strategy and tactics change, the script needs to change. Each updated version needs to be short, efficient and effective. This script is not a strategic plan but rather a note which keeps delivering on the strategic planning process.

A strategy note is a brief note that strikes a chord with each of its readers.

The strategy note is a powerful tool for leading strategy.

WRITING A STRATEGY NOTE

To create a strategy note for your firm or your client's firm, you only need to carry out six tasks.

Task 1. Write Your Recommendation
Task 2. Report Your Health
Task 3. Summarize Your Analysis
Task 4 Name Your Options
Task 5. Grow Digital Wings
Task 6. Align Your Actions

These six tasks produce a one-page communique that helps teams remember the agreed strategy and align their future actions with it. To help create a comprehensive one-pager, you may like to pick up a copy of The Strategy Note. However, I will provide a summary here.

TASK 1

In writing a one-page strategy note, the first task is to write a recommendation for the business at the top of the page.

Yes that's right. In two or three sentences, write your current recommendation for the business for the coming month or quarter. No

CHAPTER SIX: LEADING STRATEGY

analysis or considerations of alternatives are needed. At this point, write your recommendation.

Lao Tzu once wrote, "The journey of a thousand miles begins with a single step." Your recommendation provides a sense of what's next for the business from where you sit. It is important to revisit the recommendation each time another task is completed.

Three examples of recommendations might be:

'Find a regional or local supplier to reduce our over-reliance on China. Give the local supplier 40% of the sourcing of our materials.'

'Recruit secretarial support for the Board and the CFO at this time. Move a 'lack of confidence' vote in Terry Troublemaker and invite his fellow board members to request his resignation. If successful, appoint a new board member using our new diversity policy.'

'Split our agency of 350 employees into four autonomous regional service groups. Remove a layer of management. Reduce red tape, increase efficiency and enhance public value.'

STRATEGY NOTE – JUNE QUARTER

1. RECOMMENDATION

2. DEBT SCORE   QUICK SCORE   LEADER SCORE   TRIBE SCORE

3. ANALYSIS

4. OPTIONS

5. DIGITAL WINGS

6. NEXT STEPS

CHAPTER SIX: LEADING STRATEGY

TASK 2

The second task is to record four health scores.

The first two scores are the Debt-to-Equity Ratio and the Quick Ratio.

The other two scores are a leadership score and a tribe score. These scores represent a firm's trust in their leader and their leader's faith in the tribe.

Once complete, reflect on the ratios and scores. These ratios and scores move over time. Changes to the balance sheet, profit and loss statement, trust in the leadership, and faith in the tribe all impact a company's health.

- How do you feel about the four health numbers?
- Is the business's health better than ever, or has business health deteriorated in recent months or years?
- Which health scores are encouraging?
- Is the recommendation still appropriate?
- Should the recommendation be modified in light of the scores reported?
- Should the recommendation address debt, profitability, leadership, or employee performance in a more targeted way?

TASK 3

The third task is to record your analysis of the business.

Include an assessment of both the internal and external business environments. To support the analysis, you may like to create a series of appendices that contain things like projected cash flows, employee survey results, industry reports, executive reviews, market shares and industry financial ratios. If you include appendices, do so sparingly. The Strategy Note should help people move faster with influence, not engage in paralysis by analysis.

- Is the recommendation at the top of the page still appropriate?
- In light of your analysis, should the recommendation be changed?
- If needed, update the recommendation now.

TASK 4

Task four is to name the available options and highlight the best option.

Write down the best option, Plan A, in two to three sentences. Then dedicate a sentence or two for Plan B, Plan C and Plan D. Naming alternatives will serve as a blind-spot check and increase confidence

CHAPTER SIX: LEADING STRATEGY

in the preferred approach. After creating options, this may result in a new recommendation that combines two or more options.

Is the recommendation at the top of the Strategy Note still appropriate? If needed, update the recommendation now.

TASK 5

Task five is to write down the firm's ongoing commitment to growing the business digitally.

- Which older legacy IT systems should be replaced with more enabling and environmentally friendly systems?
- What value-adding commitments could be made to leading-edge technologies?
- What technologies are already being brought into the business?
- Are there AI apps or 'bots' that the business could use to enhance customer satisfaction?

In a sentence or two, name the technologies and how they add value. If the firm is not presently adopting a new aspect of technology, consider the technologies that might best support the recommendation's implementation. The Strategy Note must record an ongoing commitment to digitally advancing the business in some way.

Revisit your recommendation. Is it still appropriate?

Should you modify it in light of the digital technologies the firm is committed to adopting?

If needed, update your recommendation now.

TASK 6

The sixth and final task in writing a Strategy Note is to record the proposed action steps needed to deliver the recommendation.

Write three action steps in a way that addresses the risks of taking those actions along with ways to mitigate such risks.

Once done, revisit the recommendation at the top of the Strategy Note.

Is it still appropriate?

Great.

CHAPTER SIX: LEADING STRATEGY

CAPABILTY SIX

LEADING OTHERS

How do you grow as a leader?

If you are a leader who is focused on leading your firm's future, the ideas you have jotted down on the blank pages in this book will all help.

Whether managing the present or helping to lead the future is more important, to implement strategy, an accounting firm must build capabilities, create systems, and allocate resources to support their strategy. Leaders must continually communicate the direction via a mission or mantra hire the best people and train them to build the needed capabilities.

Communicating strategic intent repeatedly and aligning staff with it are two of the most critical tasks for a leader.

6.1 As a leader, how regularly do you convey and articulate the firm's strategy?

6.2 On the blank pages opposite, write the phrases 'trust', 'quiet confidence', 'determination' and 'expertise'. For each, jot down three things you could do to better build your people's faith in you as an honest, ethical and expert leader?

6.3 Show your list to a peer, colleague or staff member. Ask for their honest feedback – showing some new vulnerability as you do so. Repeat this exercise with two other people. Be strategic about it.

CHAPTER SIX: LEADING STRATEGY

CHAPTER SIX: LEADING STRATEGY

"People will walk through fire for a leader that is true and human."

Patrick Lencioni

FUTURE PROOF YOUR FIRM

CAPABILITY QUIZ

I created this Capability Quiz to help accountants future-proof their firms and identify areas within their professional practice that may need improvement.

Question 1. How digitally savvy are you?

A. We mostly use Excel and some unconnected software programs.
B. All our data and software is stored in the Cloud.
C. We have staff who can use and program our workflow 'bots'.
D. We have integrated AI apps into our systems.

Question 2. How ethical and sustainable is your firm?

A. We do tax and make good money from audit shield premiums.
B. We offer audit, accounting and some business advisory services.
C. We choose our clients consciously and avoid ethical dilemmas.
D. We have an ethical and sustainable competitive advantage.

Question 3. With critical thinking and problem-solving we

A. Stick to straight compliance and reporting work.
B. Help clients root out hidden costs in their businesses.
C. Consult with clients on their workforce development.
D. Understand the changing needs of our clients' customers.

Question 4. When thinking about the future

A. I trust in the past's successes
B. I hope my investments do well, or I win the lottery.
C. I have some practical measures for tracking our firm's growth.
D. We have some well-understood strategic options across our team.

Question 5. When thinking about our business's value drivers

A. I get bored or confused.
B. I know that change will be needed in the future.
C. We carry out target pricing for all our services.
D. Approaches like Focus and Differentiation excite me.

Question 6. As a leader

A. I struggle with negative evaluations of my performance.
B. I know that feedback is 'the breakfast of champions'.
C. Staff see me as a determined and humble expert.
D. My people would happily walk-through fire for me.

CAPABILITY SCORE

Calculating your Capability Score
For Q1. through Q6. Your scores are A= 1; B = 4; C= 7; D=10.

Total = Scores for Q1 + Q2 + Q3 + Q4 + Q5 + Q6

Interpreting your Capability Score

Under 20: This book could be your firm's wake-up call.

20 to 29: There is still lots of room for improvement.

30 to 39: This book can help you be more strategic, ethical and/or motivated.

40 to 49: Your firm is an inspiration to others.

Above 50: You can safely give this book to someone else.

Review your lowest scores. Investing time, resources and effort in these areas will help future-proof your firm.

CONCLUSION

Who makes your morning coffee?

Man, woman or machine?

Raelene, the barista at the vegan-friendly West End Coffee House, makes great coffee.

West End is home to Brisbane's artists and a planet conscious community. My daughter Lauren likes to meet me at 'the house' for coffee, chats and cuddles.

Raelene often jokes that it won't be long before AI and robots make the coffee.

This morning Raelene said, "You should see the new automated three-group head coffee machine we're getting next month! It will save the business time and money!"

"What about losing your job to the robot?" I asked.

"I'd love to get a Universal Basic Income."

To get a more accurate picture, I asked Raelene a series of whys.

"Why?"

"So, I can go from being a part-time to full-time volunteer."

"Why?"

"So, I can sit with old women and crochet things."

"Why?"

"Because the population is aging and there are so many lonely old people out there who have no one."

"Why?"

"Because governments and society do not have a strategy for those who are being left behind. That's why."

My series of whys helped me arrive at the megatrends of AI and ageing populations.

Lauren arrived soon after.

As an artist and children's entertainer, Lauren has mastered the art of juggling whilst walking on stilts.

CONCLUSION

I felt comforted because Lauren was working hard to keep the young ones happy, and Raelene was helping the old ones. It then occurred to me, they had left me to care for the not so old and not so young ones. With advancing AI, the slower people, including some accountants, will be left behind. But it does not have to be that way. As trusted advisors with basic income and expenditure information about their clients, accountants can become strategic.

Strategic Accountants understand that all industries become increasingly competitive and digital over time. Helping clients manage cost, quality and automation can make a big difference. Working with clients to get the right people on the bus and in the right seats also helps. As does having functional and gender inclusive teams. As we have seen, culture eats strategy for breakfast.

We have also seen that an accounting firm that is simple and not complex, regardless of its size, works well. Choosing to become a Strategic Accountant means scaling up the firm's services using a Cost Leadership, Differentiation, Focussed or Three-Sided Approach - perhaps with an added 'Right Next Door' ingredient.

Once this has been done, a Strategic Accountant can paint a similar picture for their clients.

As an artist, Raelene knows that a picture is worth a thousand words. If you pause for a moment and study the image on the back of this book, it shows a pair of juggling hands and three time-specific roles a Strategic Accountant can play.

Go on, take a peek.

The first task of analysing the past has the potential of becoming information rich.

Analysing the past begs an important question, "What is going on here?"

With greater engagement and courage, accountants can extend their services to better help their clients answer this question. If they do, they will have done 80% of the work needed to be a Strategic Accountant. Accountants with an accurate picture of what is going on will find the tasks of managing the present and creating the future much easier.

OFF WITH THE FAIRIES

My daughter Rebecca currently works for one of the top four accounting firms.

After sharing my plans for The Strategic Accountant, she shared she would not read the book.

"I love you Dad. And you are off with the fairies if you think I want to read a book that discredits my firm and portrays it as a gorilla!"

I don't blame her.

CONCLUSION

Each day, she looks for the good in her firm and she works hard to achieve the same. Despite the many crimes of the Two-Hundred-Pound-Gorilla business and modern society would fall into chaos without the good work of the top four and millions of other smaller accounting firms. However, because companies have always looked to accountants to minimise tax, the constantly shifting line between what is or isn't legal continues to beckon.

Every pound of gold a business acquires through foul means or fair means creates an imprint on that business. If the exchange has been fair and right, the resultant imprint is good. Large companies collect a multitude of imprints, both good and bad. Amazon's free shipping and customer service reputation leaves good imprints. Amazon's poor philanthropic record and its below standard working conditions leave bad imprints.[73] Most of the time, as if by magic, every pound of gold we attract comes with an ounce or two of shadow.

Some of my ancestors were Irish and grew up with the magic of fairies and leprechauns. Leprechauns are one of the fairy folk. They typically wore green suits, leather aprons and cocked hats. Each leprechaun possesses a hidden pot of gold, which he may reveal if a captor threatens him with bodily violence. Leprechauns, not unlike some accountants, are tricksters, invariably disappearing by fooling their captors into looking away.

Across the Irish Sea, at the birthplace of modern accounting, Scotland's fair folk are very sensitive creatures. One must always be honest around the fair folk, as they will know if you have lied to them. Not surprisingly, they don't take kindly to that either. They are known colloquially as faeries, but if you are superstitious, always address them as the fair folk. They have magical powers, are onlookers of human nature and are the balance between good and evil.

Faeries, tricksters and jesters have had a role in exposing sinful people and groups for centuries. Groups that generate more bad imprints than good, especially environmental ones, cause the fair folk to become upset. If we don't listen to the little people, they send death and destruction on a large scale.

As destroyers of the environment, 'The Vital Few' to eliminate first are land clearing projects, burning of coal, dirty steel production, cement production and non-electric road transport. The 'Useful Many' suggest reductions in livestock consumption, fishing trawlers, oil and gas heating, air transport and waste. Our modern world, which is filled with 8 billion people, 2 billion houses, 1.5 billion cars, 1 trillion animals slaughtered yearly, 150,000 terra-watt hours of dirty-electricity used annually and endless flights all cast a shadow.

In our modern world, despite their oaths and good intentions, many doctors kill healthy people. Some lawyers defend dishonest people who break the law. Some accountants help greedy people steal. Each profession has its gold and its shadow. A Strategic Accountant also has their gold and their shadow, which one's own jester can also discover.

CONCLUSION

SPEAKING FREELY

Comic talk show hosts Jimmy Kimmel and Stephen Colbert waged a nightly parody on Donald Trump, for his entire term as President. Kimmel made Trump the laughing-stock of America during the pandemic.

America's Top Tech CEO Tim Cook's face turned redder than an Apple at a recent Golden Globes. Comedian Ricky Gervais courted embarrassment for Cook by describing Apple's *The Morning Show* as "a superb drama about the importance of dignity and doing the right thing, made by a company that runs sweatshops in China."[74]

In the Royal Courts of England and Europe, jesters sang, told stories and performed physical comedy, acrobatics and juggling. Jesters could also give bad news to the King that no one else would dare deliver. In literature, the jester is symbolic of common sense and honesty, notably in Shakespeare's King Lear.

Jesters were permitted to speak freely to dispense frank observations and highlight the folly of the King. The irony was that a greater man could dispense the same advice and find himself being executed. Paradoxically, as the lowest member of the Court, the jester was the leader's most valued adviser, precisely because he did not strive to make the leader look good.

Many a CEO suffering from imposter syndrome will tend to pay for advice and reports that make them look good. A few years back, I completed a year-long assignment for a large law firm. In my final report to the C-Suite, I pointed out some stifling dysfunctions within their senior team. I knew that further consulting work was possible by not speaking freely. However, I placed raising the awareness of the firm's unconsciousness ahead of any future financial rewards.

As a trustworthy and frank advisor to the imposter CEO, I was not invited back.

Accountants are already trusted advisors. However, being a Strategic Accountant can be riskier. Sometimes accountants are paid well for what they know, not for the hard questions they should ask.

Strategy involves asking clients questions about what might happen and what they will do.

Offering advice on managing the present can be lost in translation and attempting to create the future can fail for many reasons. We are all wiser in hindsight. Sometimes, dodgy clients can sue advisors for what they later believe to have been ill-conceived advice. As the late Charlie Munger cautioned, "Always be careful whom you take on as a client and what you agree to."

After six years in prison, father and former Enron CFO Andy Fastow's take on ethics changed, "I was extremely greedy and lost my moral compass. The question I should have asked is not what is the rule but, what is the principle?"[75]

Fastow reflects, "In prison, you're surrounded by very violent people, very unstable people. Prisons work hard to make you uncomfortable.

But that's not what's bad about going to prison. What's bad about going to prison is that you're separated from your family."[76]

One day, your life will pass before your eyes, and you may realise that family is more important than money or gold.

Whether we are deliberate about it or not, every day, we are creating our future.

Be deliberate, ethical and intelligent when writing your playbook.

THE RETURN OF THE KING

At the start of the book, I shared a *sushi story* about a King that gave a bag of seeds to each of his three children and then left the Palace for many years.

One day, the King, tired from his travels, returned home.

The eldest son, Boris, was the first to greet the King. Boris took the King to the Treasury and opened the iron vault to reveal a foul stench of fermenting and worthless seeds.

When Donald heard of the King's return, he hastened with gold coins to purchase fresh seeds. Donald only needed to part with one gold coin to obtain a whole bag of new seeds for his father. The King was happy that his second child seemed more enterprising than the first.

The King found Jacinda carrying a basket laden with apples. Jacinda took the King by the hand and led him to a high window in the Palace.

When the King looked out, fruit trees filled the countryside.

Jacinda said, "There, Father, are your seeds."

The King named Jacinda as his heir the very next day.

After the King's death, the Royal Historian interviewed the three children.

Boris was outspoken, "As I never tire of saying, my chances of becoming PM are only slightly better than being decapitated by a frisbee, blinded by a champagne cork, locked in a fridge or being reincarnated as an olive."[77]

Donald ranted, "There was voter fraud. I should be President."[78]

When asked, Jacinda explained that, in the end, we reap what we sow.

She shared, "To me, leadership is not about necessarily being the loudest in the room, but instead, being the bridge."[79]

CONCLUSION

BRIDGING FAILURE

Being the bridge to the future is a role each of us should play in our own uniquely valuable way.

Unlike an inspirational speaker, who inspires audiences to think differently, as a motivational speaker, my role is to make sure audiences take action and create better futures. Motivational speakers are often paid more than inspirational speakers because they add more value. Strategic accounting firms like the top four are paid more than traditional firms because they add more value.

Some of the talks I give are in auditoriums filled with graduates and valedictorians. Sharing life's wisdom and offering strategies for the future with new generations is rewarding. When J.K. Rowling delivered her famous address to Harvard graduates, she shared what she feared most for herself at a young age was not poverty but failure.[80] Most accountants probably feel much the same. Less afraid of poverty and more afraid of failure.

Rowling said in her talk, "Now, I am not going to stand here and tell you that failure is fun."

Rowling notes, "Failure in life is inevitable. It is impossible to live without failing at something, unless you live so cautiously that you might as well not have lived at all – in which case, you fail by default."

As an accountant, you may never fail on the scale of Enron or Arthur Anderson, but some failure in life is inevitable. It is also possible to learn from the failure of others. One purpose of studying history is to create a better future. Indeed, those who do not look at history's failures are destined to repeat them. However, our setbacks and most significant failures can make us stronger, wiser and more humble.

THE EDGE OF TOMORROW

Back at the conference, Michael Porter looked wise. He seemed humble too. With his rounded glasses, he reminded me of an owl and an older version of Harry Potter.

The mic-runner, a little out of breath, arrived at my row in the auditorium, and the people in between passed the microphone along.

Once I thanked Porter for a thought-provoking lecture, I asked my question about shared value.

Porter had nicely pointed out in his lecture that successful collaborations between governments, NGOs, companies, and community members should be used to create shared value. Whereas traditionally, these players worked more often in opposition than in alignment. Corporations that work hard on urgent social problems alongside social sector groups

CONCLUSION

can bring together various actors to help remedy these problems. They then gain from this strategically.

Porter believed that by aiming to create greater shared value, companies could find economic opportunities that their competitors miss.

I asked Porter, "Have you given much thought about expanding the scope of shared value, where firms might take into account the needs of other non-human earthly species, like rainforests and endangered gorillas? Could this also deliver economic benefits that competitors miss?"

There was silence. Porter thought for a moment.

Then he replied, "No. But I will give it some thought. Thank you."

In closing, here's a thought.

Instead of just counting dollars, what would the future be like, if accountants learnt to juggle other planet-saving numbers?

Significant planet-saving numbers include waste recycled, water used, energy consumed, emissions produced and carbon credits. More than ever the world needs a new generation of *carbon accountants* as governments introduce increasing carbon footprint laws and taxes.

Environment Management Accounting (EMA) is maturing. EMA work reveals that 20% of the average company's operating costs represent environmentally detrimental activities. When uncovered and addressed, the embedded savings can reduce costs and save the planet.

What if all accountants reported on such environmental numbers? They would help their clients be profitable and gain competitive advantages whilst caring for our precious Earth.

The edge of tomorrow is here.

Together, let's create strategies that slow and start to reverse the extinction scenarios our children and future generations now face.

Appendix One
SEVEN BAD ACTORS

Shakespeare wrote: 'All the world's a stage, and all the men and women merely players.'

Once a business connects itself to the information superhighway or Internet, it places itself in plain sight on the world stage. Seven bad actors wait in the wings, ready to play their part in the story of an unsuspecting business. Some bad actors appear early when a business is taking off and cyber awareness is not developed. Others appear later, once a business is mature, and hard-won business assets are visible to all seven actors.

The seven bad actors are identity thieves, foreign intruders, extortionists, blackmailers, terrorists, bad apples and rotten eggs. With the right knowledge and regular investment in cyber-security, a firm can keep all seven bad actors at bay.

1. IDENTITY THIEVES

Identity thieves are the most common bad actors in our hyperconnected world of login names, passwords, credit cards and bank accounts.

Dens of identity thieves aim to obtain your personal or financial information. Once your information is obtained, it is used for personal gain, to make purchases or on-sell your identity or credit card details via the web to the highest bidder. Most identity thefts occur via phone, text, online forms or e-mail. Phone callers can be the most convincing and brazen.

APPENDIX ONE: SEVEN BAD ACTORS

For unsolicited phone callers, ask them to give you a telephone number to call them back on before you share any personal information, such as your date of birth, physical address, account information or login details. You can also contact the company they purport to work for before proceeding.

During the pandemic lockdowns, online shopping and home delivery behaviour sky-rocketed. As a result, identity thieves sent out delivery notifications via text containing malicious links, which millions of unsuspecting consumers clicked on. Delivery notification messages should not be activated but deleted instead. To track a shipment safely, log in to your customer account and check your delivery status there.

Buying via the web often requires entering name and address details into a webform, along with credit card details. Only shop online with a trusted brand from your own country or a known global brand. If a web form requests your date of birth, driver's license, or passport details, avoid that website.

Using secure transaction providers like Google Pay, Apple Pay, Pay Pal or Block when buying online may cost a little more, but knowing your credit card details are safe can be worth it.

2. FOREIGN INTRUDERS

Like ghosts stalking the corridors of your house during the night, foreign intruders steal data daily from billions of citizens' devices and business servers to increase their market or military intelligence.

Sometimes intruders are foreign intelligence services like the FBI, the China Ministry of State Security or the Russian Foreign Intelligence Service. Other times intruders are well-known corporations like Meta, Google or Microsoft.

We have some control over how much of data and activity is stolen by attending to the list below:

1. Choosing safe 'cookie' settings for website browsing. If you are unsure how to manage cookies, block them until you find out. If they are cookies from a company you trust, you may prefer to accept them.
2. Using mainstream browsers like Google Chrome and Safari allows users to search the web with relative safety.
3. Installing the latest updates, fixes and improvements for all operating systems and software apps.
4. Having antivirus prevention-detection-removal software.
5. Deploying internet monitoring firewall systems.
6. Having regular backups stored offline/offsite to isolate infected systems.
7. Replacing password-only access for multi-factor authentication mechanisms: knowledge (something only a user

knows, e.g. name of childhood pet), possession (something only a user has, e.g. their mobile device), and inherence (something only the user is, e.g. face ID or fingerprint ID).
8. Setting email filter safeguards to block all unknown, SPAM or questionable emails that contain links or attachments.
9. Educate users and provide them with Risk Assessment Tools (RATs) that allows them to report, delete and then share their experience of a phishing email, spam or scam with others. (See below Sample Email RAT).

Sample Email Risk Assessment Tool (RAT)

1.	Does the email look legitimate? It's not hard to make an email look real. Right-click on the sender's email address. Is the email address not in keeping with their brand?	EXTREME RISK	DELETE & BLOCK SENDER
2.	Does email offer business, inheritance, or romance opportunities?	EXTREME RISK	DELETE & BLOCK SENDER
3.	Does email offer a prize or question the security of your account?	HIGH RISK	DELETE & BLOCK SENDER

4.	Are you encouraged to click on an embedded link or button? Do the links look correct? Hover over them with your mouse. Does the link match the email content? Does it use the correct email domain?	HIGH RISK	DELETE & BLOCK SENDER
5.	Is there poor or unusual grammar or even a tiny error?; a sense of urgency?; use of exclamation points '!'?; a reward for doing a survey?; an offer of an investment security?; or a failure to address you personally in the greeting?	HIGH RISK	DELETE IT
6.	Does the email come from a brand you know and use?; or is the email unsolicited?	RISKY	IF IN ANY DOUBT DELETE IT

APPENDIX ONE: SEVEN BAD ACTORS

Despite all these precautions, an entire cast of foreign intruders routinely walks away largely undetected, with massive payloads of private, customer, government, sensitive commercial and mission-critical operational data.

Foreign intruders, therefore, may eventually play a role in warfare and become Terrorists:

On December 23, 2015, the Ukraine power grid cyberattack caused power outages for roughly 230,000 consumers for up to 6 hours. This cyberattack occurred during ongoing Russian military interventions in Ukraine and is attributed to a Russian advanced persistent threat group known as "Sandworm."

While conflict between NATO and Russia continues, further cyberattacks on critical infrastructure are likely.

3. EXTORTIONISTS

Extortionists steal data, wipe storage drives and deny users access to their networks and operating systems for monetary gain via ransomware attacks.

A recent Crowd Strike Report found that over two-thirds (67%) of Australian organisations suffered a ransomware attack in the previous 12 months. The global cyber extortion rate is slightly lower at 57%. In 33% of Australian cases, the extorted firm paid the ransom, costing an average of AU$1.25 million per extortion. These payments, which encourage further attacks, are often kept secret because the ransom sum is small compared to the organisation's size. Large corporates quietly pay the ransom and do not hurt their reputation by admitting they have been attacked or paid a ransom. In 2022, the Cyber Security Cooperative Research Centre (CCRC) estimated that cyber extortionists had cost the global economy US$1 trillion.

When it comes to data loss or system disablement, a defensive approach against extortion is to double or triple mirror all data across independent and completely unconnected systems. This can be a costly exercise. However, if your business is growing or mature and organisational assets are significant, redundancy in the form of multiple fallbacks and well-tested disaster recovery plans is prudent.

4. BLACKMAILERS

Blackmail is the term used to attack a person rather than an organisation. With blackmail, the sums of money involved are often less. Due in part to crypto-currency exchanges, blackmail via the Internet is rising. Most blackmailing is unreported for the same reasons that extortionists are not reported by the firms they attack.

APPENDIX ONE: SEVEN BAD ACTORS

Suppose a blackmailer sends you an email containing a photo of yourself in the shower and a video of you making love to someone you have never met. In this same email is a link to a vanishing deep website page (not searchable), where you are given instructions on how to create a bitcoin trading account - which you will use to transfer bitcoins to the blackmailer.

The blackmailer shares that they will destroy all the nude pic and the distressing video (which you conclude is a deep fake) if you transfer $30,000 worth of bitcoin to their untraceable cryptocurrency account.

How did this happen?

The blackmailer purchases your name, email and addresses online, along with thousands of others, for a small sum. The blackmailer locates you in real life. They tail you. They install a hidden camera in a public shower that you use from time to time. They film you. They remove the camera. They wait. They find a video of someone with a similar build to you and harvest a bunch of photos and dance videos of you from your social media accounts.

They make a deep fake video of you with a porn star, and voila!

What do you do?

This scenario assumes you have never broken the law or done anything you would not like to be known for publicly. If you have compromising data or photos from your past on your computer or someone else's device, that can turn up the heat once the picture is stolen.

THE STRATEGIC ACCOUNTANT

Just ask the once HRH Prince, Andrew Mountbatten-Windsor, who was pictured cuddling 17-year-old alleged sexual victim Virginia Roberts and cohabiting with convicted felons Jeffrey Epstein and Ghislaine Maxwell. On 15 Jan 2022, Andrew was stripped of his Royal Standard, all Military Honours, all Royal Patronages and no longer enjoys the HRH title.

How should you respond to a blackmailer?

Step 1. Reporting the details of the blackmail attempt is the first step. In Australia, this can be done at www.scamwatch.gov.au

Step 2. Delete the blackmailer's email and block the sender. Do not pay the ransom.

Step 3. Share your experience with others to help process your experience and raise awareness.

Step 4. Avoid future attacks by reviewing where and how you store sensitive personal data and how much of your life (data, photos, videos) can be obtained using search engines and social media apps.

Step 5. Before considering changing your email and phone numbers, check their current threat level at www.haveibeenpwned.com

5. TERRORISTS

A terrorist's primary goal is to destroy sensitive data.

No business is safe from terrorists.

Terrorist activity is usually the result of extreme ideological stances. Terrorists will destroy complete data centres and entire network systems for reasons beyond rational logic or common sense. Other times, greed can be the motivator.

An unethical competitor or rogue government agency might engage in black market cyber operations to disable and destroy entire industrial control systems or government services. A basic rule of thumb is that computers that contain valuable assets and sensitive data should never be connected to the Internet.

Malicious software (Malware) used by identity thieves, foreign intruders, extortionists, blackmailers and terrorists can't hurt your firm if your devices have never been connected to the Internet or external devices of any kind (e.g. flash sticks).

If secure computers need to run continuously, grid-independent backup batteries and power generators are required. However, there are no guarantees. Bad apples and rotten eggs also exist.

6. BAD APPLES

A bad apple employee quickly infects their neighbour.

Not all threats to your business come via the Internet. Not all bad actors are external. Bad internal actors are known as bad apples. Disgruntled employees may steal data, customer information and even intellectual property.

Knowing which employees have data access and their user privileges are essential. If you don't fully trust someone with system access, you may be sitting on a ticking time bomb.

Businesses tightly coupled to supply chain partners and contractors often share sensitive financial and customer data. Another bad apple could be a business partner's computer system. In early 2022, a Bunnings' business partner, FlexBooker, reported a data breach that exposed 3.7 million customer accounts, many of which were Bunnings customers.

Bunnings had used FlexBooker for 'click and collect' orders during the pandemic.

With customer details stolen, Bunnings customers were subject to a barrage of email and SMS scams designed to steal their identities. One Bunnings customer shared, "My phone's just blown up with these text messages all the time, and I'm scared to open up my phone because it's like, what's going to be coming at me now?"

APPENDIX ONE: SEVEN BAD ACTORS

This customer was concerned about how safe their data was and if they were more vulnerable to identity theft.

As a result of the FlexBooker breach, the customer felt forced to change their email address and then considered changing their phone number.

A bad apple quickly infects its neighbour and sometimes an entire neighbourhood.

7. ROTTEN EGGS

Rotten eggs are the last bad actors. In business, a rotten egg is the name for a terrorist inside your firm.

Despite being rare, a rotten egg, if you have one, can be lethal. There are 1.2 million poisonings from real rotten eggs each year in the United States, with 23,000 hospitalisations, and 450 deaths.

Rotten eggs create serious problems. Unlike bad apples, who steal data and information, rotten eggs work to destroy data and prevent entire systems from functioning. Rotten eggs may hook up, out of hours, in vengeful splinter groups with other rotten eggs, plotting significant acts of aggression.

A rotten egg may be an employee who has been bullied or mocked by others at some point or are withdrawn mysterious employees who get their work done with minimal engagement.

To understand your people, engage with them and maintain a sense of their personal life beyond the firm.

Appendix Two

SUCCESSFUL MERGERS & ACQUISITIONS

STRATEGY OF THE FIFTH PLAYER

Accounting firm BDO is a global network of accounting, tax, consulting and business advisory firms that provide professional services. BDO is the fifth largest accounting network globally, with one-quarter of the turnover of a typical big four firm and around twice the turnover of any of the three next firms below it.

In some ways, BDO is 'stuck in the middle.' Too big to play in a niche and often too small to play in the most significant corporate fields. However, BDO is making up ground.

Each BDO member firm is an independent legal entity in its own country. Often, individual member firms will adopt a range of more localised strategic positions, including a mixture of Differentiation, Right Next Door, Cost Leadership and Focused Differentiation.

Much of BDO's network growth comes via Mergers & Acquisitions. As a result, BDO follow the six ingredients for successful mergers and acquisitions. You may like to draw on BDO's wisdom when considering the growth or sale of your firm or when advising clients on mergers and acquisitions.

1. Assess the cultures of both the entities coming together to ensure that each has something to add to the other. Where needed, invest in new skills for all.

APPENDIX TWO: SUCCESSFUL MERGERS & ACQUISITIONS

2. Look at the value of the merger through the eyes of the clients. Make sure that 1 + 1 = 3 in terms of customer value.

3. Ensure the new structure, systems, and strategy are simple (easily understood and communicated) and scalable.

4. Have all systems and processes right to minimise or eliminate frustration from the word go.

5. Hit the ground running. Don't announce the merger or acquisition until everything is ready to go.

6. Communicate everything that has happened, is happening and is going to happen.

ENDNOTES

Introduction

1. Inaugural Australian Business Chambers' Congress, Gold Coast Convention Centre, Australia. 2011.
2. Goethe J.W., *Faust. Tragic German Play*, 1831.
3. Rowling J.K., *Harry Potter and the Order of the Phoenix*. Levine Books, 2003.
4. Adapted from Osho, *Zen, The Path of Paradox – Talks on Zen*, Vol 2, 1977.
5. Cowan W.C., Watson P.J., *The Origins of Agriculture: An International Perspective*. The University of Alabama Press. 2006.
6. Eck W., *The Age of Augustus*. Oxford: Blackwell Publishing. 2003
7. Salehi M., *A Study on the Influences of Islamic Values on Iranian Accounting Practice and Development*. Journal of Islamic Economics, Banking and Finance. 2014.
8. Pope Nicholas V., *Indulgentia*. Johannes Gutenberg Press. 1455.
9. Perks R.W., *Accounting and Society*. Chapman & Hall. 1993.
10. Brooks R., *Bean Counters: The Triumph of the accountants and How They Broke Capitalism*. Atlantic. 2019.
11. Davern M., Weisner M., Fraser N., *Technology and the future of the profession*. The University of Melbourne. 2019.
12. CA ANZ, *Capabilities for Accounting – A model for the future*. 2020.

Chapter 1

13. Hodges A., Alan Turing: *The Enigma – The Book That Inspired the Film The Imitation Game.* Penguin. *2014.*.
14. Gibbs S., *"Apple co-founder Steve Wozniak says humans will be robots' pets."* The Guardian. June 25, 2015.
15. Ziethen K., Allen A., *Juggling, the Art and its Artists.* 1985.
16. Gladwell M., *Outliers.* Little, Brown and Company. 2008.
17. Qifeng F., *Chinese Acrobatics Through the Ages.* 1985.
18. McLean B., Elkind P., *The Smartest Guys in the Room: The Amazing Rise and Scandalous Fall of Enron.* Portfolio Trade. 2003.
19. Davey M., *George Pell says some evidence Vatican officials conspired to 'destroy' him.* The Guardian. December 16, 2020.
20. Janda M., *Westpac's record $1.3 billion AUSTRAC money laundering fine explained.* ABC News. September 24, 2020.
21. Brooks R., Bean Counters: The Triumph of the accountants and How They Broke Capitalism. Atlantic. 2019.

Chapter 2

22. Mears W., *Arthur Andersen conviction overturned.* CNN Washington Bureau. May 31, 2005.
23. McLean B., Elkind P., *The Smartest Guys in the Room: The Amazing Rise and Scandalous Fall of Enron.* Portfolio Trade. 2003 .
24. Weiss B., *The Hell of the English. Associated Universities Press.1986.*
25. UK Financial Services Authority. *The Failure of the Royal Bank of Scotland.* December 2011.

26. ABN AMRO. *ABN AMRO completes legal demerger. Press release.* February 8, 2010.
27. *Agreement between NY State Dept of Financial Services and Deloitte Financial Advisory LLP.* June 18, 2013.
28. *Standard Chartered: Deloitte rejects US claims.* The Daily Telegraph. August 7, 2012
29. China Finance. *'Updated data on auditors linked with issues.'* May 23, 2013.
30. *China Hustle is the most important film of the year. Forbes Magazine.* March 30, 2018.
31. *PCAOB Announces $8 Million Settlement with Deloitte Brazil for Violations Including Issuing Materially False Audit Reports and 12 Individuals Also Sanctioned for Various Violations.* Public Company Accounting Oversight Board. December 5, 2016.
32. Segovia C., *Deloitte Construyó el Balance de Bankia en 2011 y Luego lo Auditó.* El Mundo. October 7, 2014.
33. Brooks R., *Bean Counters: The Triumph of the accountants and How They Broke Capitalism.* Atlantic. 2019.
34. Pavlov I., *Conditional Reflexes.* Oxford University Press. 1927.
35. Briloff A., *Dirty Pooling.* Accounting Review. July 1967.
36. *Seven Indicted in Westec Collapse.* New York Times. January 9, 1968.
37. McCool G., *Accounting firm Ernst & Young was sued by New York prosecutors over allegations it helped to hide Lehman Brothers' financial problems, in the first major government legal action stemming from the Wall Street company's 2008 downfall.* Business News NY. December 22, 2010.
38. Brooks R., *Bean Counters: The Triumph of the accountants and How They Broke Capitalism.* Atlantic. 2019.

39. Paine L., *Ethics: A Basic Framework*. Harvard Business School Background Note 307-059. 2006.
40. Patrick A., *KPMG meets the Leadership Paradox*. Australian Financial Review. February 12, 2021.
41. Ibid.
42. Marriage M., *KPMG's 'stop moaning' boss steps aside*. Financial Times. February 11, 2021.
43. *A History of Cooper Brothers & Co. 1854-1954*. Garland Publishers.1986.
44. PwC Worldwide Annual Report 2001- Income includes banking and capital markets, investment management and insurance.
45. Brooks R., *Bean Counters: The Triumph of the accountants and How They Broke Capitalism*. Atlantic. 2019.
46. Ibid.
47. King A., Tandros E., *PwC, KPMG break $3m per partner barrier*. Financial Review. October 21, 2015.
48. Vanian J., *Apple Co-Founder Steve Wozniak Talks Innovation, Microsoft, and Being Introverted*. Fortune Magazine. April 21, 2017.

Chapter 3

49. Suarez J., *Three Experts on Quality Management: Philip B. Crosby, W. Edwards Deming, Joseph M. Juran*. Department of the Navy TQL Office.1992.
50. Cirillo R., *The Economics of Vilfredo Pareto*. Frank Cass & Co. 1978.
51. *Five Whys Technique*. Asian Development Bank. February 2009.
52. Velmurugan M., *The Success and Failure of Activity-Based Costing Systems*. Journal of Performance Management, 23.2 (2010): 3–33. March 15, 2012.

53. Duke J., *Female CEOs, directors boost company values*. Sydney Morning Herald. June 19, 2020.

Chapter 4

54. Kaplan R., Norton D., *The Balanced Scorecard: Translating Strategy into Action*. HBS Press.1996
55. Lencioni P., *Silos, Politics and Turf Wars. Wiley, 2006.*
56. Lencioni P., *The Advantage: Why Organizational Health Trumps Everything Else in Business.* Jossey-Bass. 2012.
57. Hale J., *The Strategy Note.* Ingram. 2020.
58. Ibid.
59. Ford J., Mantica G., Ristow G., *The Arnol'd Cat: Failure of the Correspondence Principle.* Physica D, Volume 50, Issue 3, July 1991, p 493–520.
60. Brandenburger A., Nalebuff B., *The Rules of Co-opetition.* Harvard Business Review. January 2021.
61. Sakurazaka H., *All You Need is Kill.* 2004. The screenplay *Edge of Tomorrow* adapted from the book.
62. Hale J., *The Strategy Book.* Ingram. 2020.

Chapter 5

63. Pearce E., Stringer C., Dunbar R., *New insights into differences in brain organisation between Neanderthals and anatomically modern humans.* Proceedings Royal Society of Biological Sciences. 2013.
64. Hale J., *The Strategy Book.* Ingram. 2020.

65. Magretta J., *Understanding Michael Porter - The Essential Guide to Competition and Strategy*. HBS Press. 2012.
66. Porter M., *Competitive Strategy - Techniques for Analysing Industries and Competitors*. HBS Press. 1998.
67. Miller J., *Buffett: Enron has silver lining*. Chicago Tribune. 2002.
68. Ibid.
69. Isidore C., *Ford's Mustang Mach E is eating into Tesla's US sales*. CNN Business. March 5, 2021.
70. Porter M., *Competitive Strategy - Techniques for Analysing Industries and Competitors*. HBS Press. 1998.

Chapter 6

71. Lencioni P., *The Five Dysfunctions of a Team*. Jossey-Bass. 2002.
72. Plenert G., *Discover Excellence – An Overview of the Shingo Model and its Guiding Principles*. CRC Press. 2018.

Conclusion

73. Hanbury M., *Jeff Bezos boasts in letter to shareholders that 40 million Americans make less than any Amazon employee*. Business Insider Australia. April 16, 2020.
74. *Ricky Gervais slams Apple over Chinese factories*. BBC News. January 6, 2020.
75. Elkind P., *The Confessions of Andy Fastow*. Fortune Magazine. July 1, 2013.
76. Ibid.

ENDNOTES

77. Boris Johnson.
78. Donald Trump.
79. Jacinda Ardern.
80. www.news.harvard.edu/gazette/story/2008/06/text-of-j-k-rowling-speech

ACKNOWLEDGEMENTS

I have learned the value of good accounting from many people. My uncle Peter Hale is a Chartered Accountant. Uncle Pete introduced me to basic concepts like assets, liabilities and depreciation when I was just a lad. When I first started out in strategy consulting over two decades ago, I was befriended by Bob McInnes, a Chartered Accountant from Casino, a small regional centre in New South Wales. Over many years, Bob referred his clients to me, so I could assist them with their strategy.

In recent years I have been assisted by a wonderful group of accounting professionals in Queensland. I am thankful to accounting colleagues, Bryan Worn, Dale Edwards, Natasha Milne, Natalie Kidcaff and Susan Rix. A special thanks also to Oscar Saez and the wonderful team at Cengage Learning Australia for their ongoing support with learning materials for my writing and Executive Education work.

I am also grateful to friends and family for their willingness to read early drafts of *The Strategic Accountant* and offer generous feedback: James Carlopio, Judith Bennett, Oscar Hauptman, Dolores Cummins, Jane Oliver, Brad Reece and Tom Smith. Finally, I would like to thank my youthful parents Bob and Jan Hale and my precious wife, Johanna Hale for their continued support of my journey as a writer, both on and off the page.

ABOUT THE AUTHOR

John Hale is the founder of Hale Consulting Group, a globally focused management consulting firm specialising in strategy, people and change. As a motivational speaker, John has delivered over a thousand talks in twelve countries across four continents, to leaders from Fortune 500 and mid-sized companies to start-ups and public sector organisations. John has also worked as an early stage investor and advisor. He has been a Visiting and Adjunct Professor and has taught in five business schools, including Singapore Management University, Bond University and Melbourne Business School.

As a young child, John grew up in the developed and developing world. Living in both patriarchal and matrilineal cultures grounded him in the need for truth and justice as well as the ethics of care and co-operation. John brings a balance of sense and sensibility to his work. He currently resides in Australia.

Hale Consulting Group
VALUE DRIVEN STRATEGIES

Hale Consulting Group is dedicated to helping organisations of all kinds drive value through better strategy, leadership and corporate wellbeing.

Please visit our website and explore

Keynote Speaking: John Hale shares value-driven ideas and strategies with thousands of leaders each year at global forums, national conferences and company events.

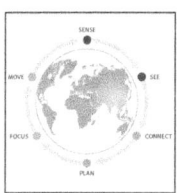

Consulting: HCG Consultants deliver strategy and organisational assignments for corporate, industry and professional groups, across a variety of industries in various parts of the globe.

Leadership Mentoring: HCG Consultants provide expert mentoring programs that empower leaders and help organisations advance in healthy ways.

www.halecg.com +61 407 301 200

www.ingramcontent.com/pod-product-compliance
Lightning Source LLC
Chambersburg PA
CBHW070254010526
44107CB00056B/2453